These Things You Shall Do... AND GREATER

The Physics of Change

GREG SIMMONS

Mulai De Guise
PUBLISHING

"Drink no longer water, but use
a little wine for thy stomach's sake."

1 Timothy v. 23.

These Things You Shall Do... AND GREATER

The Physics of Change

GREG SIMMONS

Mulai De Guise
PUBLISHING

These Things You Shall Do
...AND GREATER

ISBN # 0-615-13386-X
Mulai de Guise Publishing, LLC.
P.O. Box 380
Rainier, Washington 98576
SAN # 851-8440
Telephone: (360) 740-8278
Toll Free: (866) 922-8278
Fax: (360) 740-9182
www.mulaideguisepublishing.com

'Tis writ, "In the beginning was the Word."
I Pause, to wonder what is here inferred.
The Word I cannot set supremely high:
A new translation I will try.
I read, if by the spirit, I am taught,
This sense, "In the beginning was the Thought."

Goethe

CONTENTS

CONTENTS

ACKNOWLEDGMENTS

It is very difficult to estimate or to understand the magnitude of someone's contribution to your life when it cannot be compared to anything else relative. My life was lived in a way that I thought was ideal, and until it was turned upside down so that I could get a better view, I would never have known how to do that for myself. It is in this regard that I dedicate these writings to a magnificent being, Ramtha, the Enlightened One.

My sincere thanks to JZ Knight, whose fortitude and commitment to these teachings has held this ship together on many a stormy night.

I want to thank my wife and children for unselfishly allowing me to be away from home for so much of the last eight years. I never felt as if I shouldn't continue this work even though there were many "sleepovers" that I missed with my children.

I wholeheartedly thank those who helped me with this book, which includes Nancy and Elena at Beyond the Ordinary Webcast radio, Pat Richker for her uncompromsing help and meticulous proofreading, Jaime Leal-Anaya for his readiness to help keep this book in momentum, to Shelley Lucas for her artistic mind, to Stephanie Millham who made the book better by putting final touches in the book, and to Laura Craig for her enthusiasm, expertise, support, and friendship.

I want to acknowledge the students of the Great Work. the most courageous people I have ever met, who have sacrificed a casual life for a journey of adversity and continuous challenge. I am honored to be a part of a worldwide student body that has realized that the world has little to offer and that greater realities continue to beckon us all.

FOREWORD

"Given the results of scientific research, the conclusion that consciousness creates the physical universe through the process of observation is inescapable."

Dr. Larry Farwell
Harvard-trained physicist

I have always had a fascination for the improbable. I loved reading about the extraordinary beings in *Autobiography of a Yogi* and *Life and Teachings of the Masters of the Far East* while dreaming about being that adept in developing my mind over the laws of matter. It would take another twenty-five years before I began to develop similar abilities.

I landed at the South African city of Johannesburg in the winter of 2000 to facilitate a weeklong Retreat for Ramtha's School of Enlightenment (RSE) to students wanting to learn to be responsible for their own lives and to develop their mind over matter. I immediately went to the Hertz car rental counter to pick up my reserved car. I said, "My name is Mr. Simmons and I am here to pick up my car." The agent said, "Certainly, sir. Fill out this form and I will see if your car is ready."

I began filling out the form with my name, address, company name, and so on until I came to the three boxes where I was to accept or decline the insurance and to initial the boxes appropriately. In a moment my brain calculated and silently voiced the following information. It reminded me that I had not been in a car accident since I was eighteen years old. It continued to remind me that I had not even had a moving traffic violation for over two decades. It quickly calculated the savings to the company if I declined the insurance. When I still hesitated, it reminded me that I was a master in an Ancient

School of Wisdom that had taught me how to create my day, and it assured me that no such ominous reality was in the mix for that day.

I declined the insurance, checked the appropriate boxes, and handed the form to the agent. He separated the form into its three copies. He took the pink copy and put it into an envelope, handed me the keys to the car and said, "Have a nice day!"

I walked out the double doors at the end of the hall into an enormous underground parking garage. On the way to our car I asked Kim, the lady who organizes our South African events, to drive us to the hotel. We got into the van, and before she got out of the garage she crunched the van against a concrete wall. I was in shock. All I could do was see myself back at the Hertz counter listening to that voice telling me about being a master in the school of blah, blah, blah and nothing ominous being in my immediate future. I just closed my eyes and wondered what I had been thinking at that counter. Kim backed up and continued to scrape the side of the van before pulling out and leaving the airport garage.

When we got to the hotel I told Kim that I would talk to her the next day so that we could take care of this unexpected development. I went into the hotel and went to sleep. The next morning I was out in the lobby looking for Kim so that we could resolve this matter that was weighing heavily on my mind. As it turned out, she was busy all day finalizing the logistics for the upcoming event.

By the time I was ready to go to bed that night, I knew that I was going to have to take care of this situation myself. I sat up in my bed before I went to sleep and moved my awareness to a part of my brain that has access to the past, present, and future, a simple technique that I had learned at the Ramtha school. In my mind I went back to the airport, walked back up to the Hertz rental counter, and met with the same agent. I said, "My name is Mr. Simmons and I am here to pick up my car." He said, "Certainly, sir. Fill out this form and I will see if your car is ready." I filled out my name, address, and company name. When I came to the insurance option, I immediately accepted the insurance and initialed all three boxes. He separated the form, put the pink copy in the envelope, gave me the keys and said, "Have a nice day." In my mind I said, "You don't know how nice a day I am going to have." I walked out the office through the double doors into the underground garage and then immediately came out of my focus.

The whole process took about three minutes. The next day I saw Kim as she came to the hotel to finalize some last-minute details. I asked her if she had contacted Hertz and she said, "Oh, yes, I talked to them yesterday." I think she was finished with her comment when I anxiously asked, "And what did they say?" She said, "I asked the agent to check on our insurance, as we had had a little accident." I reminded her that "we" didn't have a little accident. She had the accident! However, after looking up our rental agreement, the agent said not to worry, that we were fully covered. Kim told me the agent's final comment was, "He signed in all the right places."

I was so excited, not because I didn't have to pay Hertz, though that was a relief, but because this outcome was the result of a focused intent. I had become what I wanted to experience. In our school we call this an analogical moment. In an analogical moment, everything is possible. This incredulous outcome was made possible by my knowledge of quantum observation. "Quantum observation is not a process of passively perceiving something that is already there. It is an act of creation, an act of manifesting concrete reality from abstract potential." This is a quote from a Harvard-trained physicist.

I had a greater understanding of the plasticity of reality and the secret of how to use my brain to develop my mind over the laws of matter. I knew that the true spiritual journey was all about this analogical moment, its pursuit, and that this state of mind was the mind that the masters of the Far East and those in *Autobiography of a Yogi* were able to achieve.

The analogical moment is that quintessential experience that allows the sorcerer (one who is adept at accessing the source) to move in the realm of all possibilities. All great beings pursue this moment. It is so elusive that you will not know you have achieved it until you have finished being it. However, you will notice its obvious effects in your life. It is in this realm that the impossible becomes probable.

This book is a record of my understanding and experience of the nature of reality. It is an account of the power of an analogical moment and its basis in the true spiritual journey.

Greg Simmons
Tokyo, Japan, one day before presenting this extraordinary knowledge to a new group of students.

"There is nothing more sterling
than to watch a human being do the impossible."

Ramtha

Chapter 1

A Few Minutes to Weave a Dream of Possibilities

Since 1999 I have given many presentations to various groups of people in over twenty countries. These groups ranged greatly in number and interest. There were only two women who showed up in Calais, France, and even with moderate translation they seemed to understand the importance of the message. There was only one young lady in Edinburg, Scotland, and she showed up twenty minutes late. In 1999 in Johannesburg, South Africa, and in 2003 in Antwerp, Belgium, there were audiences of 400 who attended the presentation. The purpose of these presentations is to provide such compelling information that those listening are inspired to register for a weeklong Retreat or, in the very least, to want to know more about the school and the teachings of Ramtha. It is a formidable challenge. In ninety minutes a tapestry of possibilities must be weaved.

I begin the presentation by telling the audience that I am one of Ramtha's appointed teachers and over the past eight years we have been presenting information in a weeklong Retreat setting. I tell those at these presentations that if they want to have the greatest week of their life, so far, that this Retreat exponentially increases their chances of that happening. I know that this statement is edgy and arrogant enough to keep the attention of the audience.

I began gathering this evidence during the third year of what had come to be called Ramtha's World Tour. It was evident from the very beginning that these trainings produced extraordinary results and that the informal feedback was overwhelmingly positive, but to what statistical degree it was effective was not yet known.

I devised a simple questionnaire with the following options:
1) The Retreat was worth my investment of the time and money.
2) The Retreat was worth my investment and I would recommend it to a friend.
3) The Retreat was one of the top five events of my life.
4) The Retreat was the greatest week of my life, so far.

The questionnaires were handed out and the participants were asked to check off the statement that most closely resembled their experience. The first questionnaire was handed out to the participants in Australia in 2001. It was not handed out at a particularly high emotional point in the training to ensure better results. It was handed out toward the end of the event to the one hundred students who had spent the previous week learning how to consciously create a lifestyle of their own choosing. Eighty-four percent of those students from Australia reported that it was the greatest week of their life, so far. I was stunned and pleased. This documented statistic has never been lower than the initial eighty-four percent for all the years that have followed.

Now I tell the audience that in the next ninety minutes I will explain why this Retreat is valued so highly by those who attend.

It is commonly known that science has been telling us for the past ten to fifteen years that we use less than ten percent of our brain. What they didn't tell us was how much less than ten percent we use. As it turns out, we use less than two percent. When scientists mapped the human genome several years ago, they reported that humans were only expressing one to two percent of their DNA capabilities, which is a shocking statistic and correlates exactly with the percentage of usage for our brain. The reason that students who attend these Retreats report that it is the greatest week of their life, so far, is because they learn how to access more of their brain and the parts of their brain that have a greater capability for producing what it is they want.

The part of the brain that we use ninety-eight to ninety-nine percent of the time is called the neocortex. It is the large, upper portion of the brain. Its primary function is to continuously assess the environment and make decisions that ensure the safety of the body. For example, it is the part of the brain that reminds you to look both ways before crossing a street. It will also interfere with your thinking when you are standing on a cliff overlooking a beautiful vista. It will suggest that today is not a good day to try flying and that more information is needed to consider this option. It has the survival of the organism as its highest priority. Although this is a valued quality for long life, it has its limitations in regard to a true spiritual journey.

The neocortex has a bias towards new opportunities. If this part of the brain cannot predict the outcome of a new dream, goal, or novel circumstance, it automatically objects to any further consideration. In other words, opportunities that involve an unknown outcome will never get the support from the part of the brain that we use ninety-eight to ninety-nine percent of the time. Unexpected wealth, an instantaneous remission of a disease, an unusual business opportunity, or a potential new romance outside your cultural comfort zone are all considered highly risky to the neocortex.

How many opportunities, no matter how promising, have you lost because this decision-making part of your brain could not predict the impact of a new opportunity on your current life?

My first job after graduating from college was to work for a large social service agency in New York City. Part of its service was to relocate foster children from the ghettos of New York to an upper middle-class neighborhood forty-five minutes away in Westchester County. Westchester is an exclusive county, including towns such as Larchmont, New Rochelle, and Scarsdale. These foster children were driven from Jerome Avenue in the Bronx to White Plains, New York. They were shown the public school, a two-block walk on sidewalks under a tree-lined street. The community center was state of the art with basketball courts, a pool, and soccer fields.

Several weeks after their visit, each of these children were given the opportunity to move to this new neighborhood. Without exception, they each said "No thanks." These were children that slept with long sticks next to their beds. Each night, as the lights were turned out in the apartment, rats would move down the halls looking for carelessly dropped bits of food, and if they made their way into the bedrooms, the children had a weapon for defense. It was this drastic environment that the children of the Bronx chose over relocating forty-five minutes away to an upper middle-class neighborhood.

The part of the brain that you and I use ninety-eight to ninety-nine percent of the time to make our critical life decisions is the same part of the brain that the children of the Bronx used to miss an opportunity that could have dramatically changed their lives.

The reason that the students of these Retreats value it so highly is that they learn how to access the different parts of their brain that have a much greater capability of giving them what they want. Having this ability substantially adds to the quality of their lives.

The part of the brain that sits under the neocortex is called the midbrain. The midbrain has access to the past, present, and future. Remember the Hertz car rental story? The part of the brain that I accessed for that three-minute focus was the midbrain. In this part of the brain, you can go to the past and change any situation in which you wished you had made a different choice. If you are successful in attaining this analogical moment with that new choice as your focus, then your current life will reflect that change. It is also this part of the brain that continuously sends you impressions of your immediate future. When you learn to relax the neocortex and its constant evaluation of the environment, your awareness automatically moves into the midbrain. There is a technique taught at the Retreats for doing this. "Be still and know that you are God" is the biblical reference for attaining this state of presence.

In December 1997, I am about to pay for a train ticket from Northern India to Varanasi, a twelve-hour train ride. I tell the ticket agent that I want a sleeper car with all the amenities. He asks me if I want A/C and I reply, "Of course not, it is December." The agent smiles and issues me a ticket. I go to my car and to my surprise and shock it has four bunk beds with only wire springs as a cushion. Before I can complain to the conductor, the train begins to move and I quickly jump into my compartment.

This train, as I come to find out later, is called a commuter train and stops anyplace an Indian is sitting under a tree or standing by the tracks. This train never reaches its cruising speed during the first eight hours of daylight. However, it is now dark and I have taken every piece of clothing out of my backpack and placed it somewhere, anywhere, on my body. I am huddled in a fetal position on the springs of the upper berth trying to stay warm. I know that heat rises and I am hoping the upper bunk will help. I am desperate. I have completely forgotten everything I knew about being a master that has control over its body. I am in pure survival. It turns out to be a very long night.

Just after the sun comes up and begins to warm the compartment, the train again begins its incessant stopping at every opportunity to pick up another customer. At one of these stops, a gentleman opens my compartment door and sits down across from me. After a short time he speaks to me in perfect English and asks where I am going. I inform him, after my account of the Train Ride From Hell, that I am going to Varanasi. He tells me he works for the railroad and proceeds to educate me regarding A/C, which means "Conditioned Air," cold air in the summer and warm air in the winter. But his greatest piece of information was to inform me that behind this train is an express train that would get me to Varanasi much quicker and I can get on it at the next major stop, only three hours up the line. "Oh, my God," I said in great relief. I was once again feeling like a master in full control of my destiny. I quickly queried him about this express train and its services. After being assured it was all I had hoped the first train ride would be, I was now fully prepared to enjoy the remainder of my trip to Varanasi. It was during these next three hours that my destiny was tenuous. Unbeknown to my conscious awareness (the thoughts of the neocortex), I was being sent information of my immediate future. Because I was relaxed with noplace to go, I was able to receive these messages even though they were not completely literal. Often they come as hunches or gut feelings. There are documented scientific studies that refer to this "second" brain that is located in the stomach.

When my stop came to get off this Train Ride From Hell, the gentlemen from the railroad company told me that my bad karma was over and this was the stop to transfer to the express train. In a most counterintuitive response, I told him that I had decided to stay on this train that I knew would take another twelve hours to arrive in Varanasi. He looked at me as if I had lost all rationale. I didn't even budge from my seat to look at the modern train station. In a moment the train began its slow but continuous journey to Varanasi. I arrived at midnight and quickly found a hotel.

The next morning I awoke to the news that the express train to Varanasi that I did not get on had crashed and killed fifty-five people. I sat up in my bed and spent a few quiet moments reflecting on my choice to stay with the Train Ride From Hell and realized once again the expanded capabilities of the midbrain and the gift that knowledge can offer.

The last major portion of the brain is called the cerebellum and sits in the rear of the skull underneath the neocortex. The ancient term for this part of the brain is called the Observer. Interestingly enough, its function is exactly as that of the contemporary definition of the Observer in quantum physics. The Observer in quantum physics affects the outcome of any experiment according to the expectation of the Observer. In other words, two scientists running the exact same experiment will record different results according to their own expected results.

The reason this is so important is that it puts full responsibility of the quality of life in the hands of each of us as the Observer. Mainstream science has documented this concept with a 99.8 percent probability that consciousness has a direct effect on our life, and these studies were conducted by Dr. Larry Farwell, a Harvard-trained physicist.

It is this part of the brain that is connected to all information and called the quantum field in physics. I listened as one of the RSE teachers talked about Albert Einstein, who at twelve years old asked the following question: If I ride my bicycle at the speed of light and I turn on my headlamp, will I see the light? Einstein was not a great student in school. He was a patent clerk in a Swiss office, but because he had contemplated this question for ten years he received the information that allowed him to develop his famous theories of relativity and special relativity. At the time of his contemplations, there were no professors giving lectures on the special properties of light and there were no papers written or submitted to scientific journals that he could have read on that subject . So where did Einstein get his information that led to his famous theories? As you will learn at the Retreats, this part of the brain is connected to all knowledge, and if you can ask the right question and use the brain properly you can know anything.

Is there irrefutable scientific proof that what you think affects the quality of your life? Is there a scientific basis for creating intentional reality? The answer is YES, with a 99.8 percent probability. This probability is as certain as the apple that will fall from the tree. In other words, the probability that consciousness has a direct effect on your life is as certain as the laws of gravity.

This part of the brain called the Observer is the lower cerebellum and functions like the lamp on a slide projector. This lamp is always illuminated and has a bulb that is guaranteed for a lifetime. It projects on the screen (your life) whatever slide (neuronet) you have placed in the projector. To change your life you must choose a different slide and insert it into the projector. This simplistic analogy is in complete compliance with current quantum theory. Wave/particle phenomena (reality) appear and the attributes they display are affected by how, when, and where the Observer chooses to make an observation.

This knowledge of the Observer has been preserved as a thread of truth throughout history. The great Gothic cathedrals of Europe were constructed in stone so that this knowledge could not be easily manipulated or translated according to interpretation. Fulcanelli, in his great work *Le Mystère des Cathédrals*, explains the construction of these cathedrals so that knowledge would transcend time and personal interpretation. The stained-glass windows of these monumental structures are a reminder that when the sun (Observer) shines through the windows that the pattern of those windows (neuronet) is projected on the cathedral floor (the landscape of one's life). This is a reminder of the function of the Observer and how it is always collapsing probabilities into reality according to the expectation of the Observer.

There are thousands of documented scientific tests that validate that conscious intention has a direct effect on your life, but no experiments have been more dramatic than those done in 1995 by French researcher René Peoch. By using a random event generator (REG) dressed up as a chicken, Dr. Peoch wanted to see if day-old baby chicks could affect random events. A REG is a sophisticated coin-toss machine. It is designed so that if there are 50,000 events (coin tosses), the machine will respond 25,000 times one way (heads) and 25,000 times the opposite way (tails). The more events in the experiment, the closer the machine will respond fifty percent one way and fifty percent the other way.

The REG dressed as a large chicken was introduced to the day-old baby chicks and through imprinting, these chicks bonded with the REG as if it were their mother. This machine, which was only capable of turning left or right, was sent down a long hall to where the baby chicks could see it coming. As the REG machine approached, the baby chicks began to chirp and continued chirping as long as the machine was in sight. At the end of the trials, the calculations were tallied. In seventy-five percent of the cases the machine turned toward the baby chicks while turning away only twenty-five percent. This is a major and significant deviation from randomness. If day-old baby chicks can influence a machine, imagine the effect a brain can have on its environment if it is properly used.

Knowledge is the most important ingredient for having options regarding the quality of your life. Without knowledge, people are relegated to the skills they have and can only imagine so much with limited knowledge.

I have just returned home from an evening financial seminar. In the packet of handouts is a $1,000,000 laminated bill. It looks real enough. My five-year-old son sees the bill and his eyes get really big. "Is it real?" he asks, and I say, "What if it is? What would you buy with it?" He tells me about these two toys he has been wanting. When he finishes describing them to me, I say, "Is that it?" He assures me he is satisfied with his "big" purchases. Now let me ask you a question: Do you have more knowledge than my son? Could you spend more of that $1,000,000 because you have more knowledge? How about spending all of it in a few minutes? That is an example of the utility and the power of knowledge.

This is the presentation that is given that asks those in attendance if they can see how their life would be significantly better if they could learn how to properly use their brain.

"It is remarkable that so little of our life
is taken up with important moments."

Anna and the King

Chapter 2

THE TRUE SPIRITUAL JOURNEY

How does one begin this journey? I am featured on Web Radio every third Thursday of the month on www.beyondtheordinary.net. The program is called *Ask Dr. Greg,* and for the past twenty-four months I have had a chance to answer questions from listeners around the world. This next question is a good beginning for the understanding of the true spiritual journey. The question comes from a listener in Turkey.

"I read the *White Book* of Ramtha in the Turkish language. I have been impressed by Ramtha's ideas. I have to explore in this area. I live in Turkey. I am a Muslim. I want to learn the comments of Ramtha about Islamism. Why did not Ramtha discuss anything about Mohammed and Islamism in the *White Book*? I want to learn a lot of things on the school of enlightenment. Which way must I follow to begin my enlightenment?"

To begin the journey of enlightenment requires a person's desire to want to know more. In the mid eighties, before I turned forty years old, I had reached a level of success within the criteria of my own definition of success. I owned three homes that included an ocean-view condo in Southern California, a ski house at Lake Tahoe in Nevada, and a large oceanfront home in Washington State. I had investments in Arabian horses, bank stock, and was coeditor of a newly published book. I had a six-figure income that would have become over $1,000,000 a year within three years. In my own mind I had reached the pinnacle of success, but with all of this success I was continuously asking the question: "There must be something more." It was this contemplation that led me on my true spiritual journey and a permanent move to the Pacific Northwest and my study with Ramtha.

Ramtha's philosophy and truth is 35,000 years old. He came long before Mohammed, Jesus, and Buddha. His teachings go back to the foundations of Earth and the history of the cosmos. Therefore this knowledge predates all religions. All "isms" — Catholicism, Judaism, Islamism, or any of the Christian "isms" — came long after ancient wisdom. All religions are personal interpretations by men claiming to be messengers of God. If that were true, then we must surmise that God had different messages at different times. That sounds suspiciously inconsistent. It sounds more like an interpretation for political and personal power. We don't have to go back too far in history to see the atrocities of the Catholic Church and what was done to those who did not believe in the "word of God" according to St. Paul.

All "isms," all religions, and all philosophies are interpretations of truth. The teachings of Ramtha are an account of the history of the cosmos and humanity's journey in it. These concepts were not taught to gain political or religious power. They were known long before politics and religion were invented. Therefore from this view can you see why Ramtha did not mention Mohammed? I do not think that Ramtha has much respect for religions or the leaders of those religions that separate God from man or any organizations that hold women as less than equal to men. As Ramtha has said, "Even the Buddhists do not allow women to be the Dalai Lama."

Neither Buddhism, the Catholic Church, nor Christianity follow in the footsteps of their leaders. The Buddhists are celibate. We know that Prince Siddhartha was a husband and a father. Wouldn't the Buddhists have a better understanding of their beloved leader if they emulated his life more closely? Jesus was called Rabbi. A Rabbi in biblical times was a married man. It was necessary for the Jewish clergy to be married so they could also counsel in secular matters. According to Ramtha, Sir Laurence Gardner, Dan Brown, and many other contemporary scholars, Jesus was not only married but was the father of two children. His wife was Mary Magdalene, and their two children started the lineage of the sovereign houses of Europe.

This is how far religion has deviated from the truth and its documented history. The first step in pursuing enlightenment is to desire to want to know more. If you hold that contemplation, the door of opportunity for that journey to enlightenment will open. It did for Einstein and it will for you. This is as certain as the laws of gravity!

"Women who seek to be equal with men
lack ambition."

Timothy Leary
American psychologist

Chapter 3

The Theater(s) of Reality

Reality is stranger than fiction. What if science is telling us the same thing Shakespeare told us a few hundred years ago: "Life is but a stage full of sound and fury signifying nothing." Fortunately, science is not saying this but rather something even more bizarre. Imagine for a moment that each of us is the director, writer, producer, and stagehand for our own life's play and every day we go to the theater and rehearse our next scene. If we want to change the scene and rewrite it so that it takes on another line of potential, we have the same authority that the director has to do this.

There is not one aspect of this play that we do not control. What science is saying is that this is how we construct reality and we do it every day at our theater. A parallel reality is simply a script or character change that is playing simultaneously at the theater next door. There are an infinite number of theaters all in a row that are playing all of the potential rewrites. You only need to put your attention on the theater that is playing the new script that you now wish to experience. This is the Many-Worlds Theory.

If you remember the story of the Hertz car rental, I simply rewrote the script according to my new desire and watched it play out in my mind (rehearsal). The next day the theater was open to the public and played that scene to a full house.

There is not one aspect of your life that you cannot rewrite and, equally encouraging, you can rewrite scenes from the past and replay the new sequel that will have astounding repercussions on your current reality. If there are circumstances or situations from your past in which you still suffer the consequences of those choices today, you can change all of it.

If you understand how to move consciousness to the midbrain, then you are in control of rewriting those circumstances where you wish you had made a better choice. Remember, the midbrain has access to the past, present, and future. In this state of mind, you are rewriting a past circumstance in the presence of the Now. To the brain, the presence defines the only script that was ever used. If you learn to do this successfully, your life will not have to continue to suffer the consequences of those earlier choices.

In the Retreats, students always ask if they can erase the memory of a difficult divorce or the painful loss of a loved one. These are deep, emotional experiences and it takes a student of great ability to do this. My answer is more in line with a beginning student's level of acceptance. Therefore rather than erase the experience, they are asked to rewrite their emotional response to that particular circumstance or situation. If they can rewrite the scene that reflects their being older and wiser, then the relationships that were fractured from before will be magically mended. The greatest healing will take place within the one who has rewritten the script to reflect the wisdom of this knowledge. This works like magic, because in the analogical moment of creating this reality the brain records the incident as if it were the one and only time that this circumstance happened. As our Harvard-trained physicist continues to remind us, "Reality is only as valid as its last observation," and changing the past is the last observation.

"If I shift to a new timeline and others still recall my past, does that mean that I have not shifted? I smoked but now I don't, but some people recall that I did. If all of this is linear thinking, can that mean that there are many of me and I am only where I place my consciousness? If that is

so, then am I interacting with people who are not there at all in their own consciousness but purely and simply only reflecting myself?"

It is a quantum postulate that simply says there are as many options of each of us as can be imagined and that they all exist simultaneously. When I changed the way I observed the Hertz rental agreement, I moved into a parallel reality that reflected that action.

It is my fervent truth that the people, places, things, times, and events in each of our lives reflect our own expectations. The moment we change, so does our environment. It does it seamlessly with a history that supports the new reality. We move seamlessly in our dreams and it all makes sense. It is this same seamlessness that is experienced with the shifting of timelines.

When we shift timelines, those people in our new reality will play the part that is consistent with the content of that new environment. If we have changed from smoking to nonsmoking and have done it flawlessly, no one in the new reality with have a relationship with us as a smoker. When we find people who are still relating to us in the old reality, we can be certain that we are still in the transitional phase. This simply means that we are walking in both worlds without being fully committed to either. Eventually one will become dominant and we will be fully in that reality.

"Is there accountability with having committed crimes? If you can successfully shift timelines from being a thief to an honest person, then who is to judge which of those two personalities you should be responsible for?"

You can only be responsible for the personality that you are currently occupying. You will not have a conscious history of the other personality. Some people will say that this could be used as a rationale for devious behavior, but it is very unlikely that a devious or immoral person would have the knowledge, the skill, or the determination to shift timelines. This move requires a state of analogical intent, and to exercise this level of mastery requires that the person operate from a very pure state of mind. So this ability has a built-in safeguard. When you learn to move elegantly from one neuronet in the brain to another, the new neuronet has its own congruent history and you will not remember that it was ever any other way.

In the story of the Hertz car rental, the Many-Worlds Theory is the knowledge I used to make that change without feeling any concern regarding Hertz and their financial loss. When confronted by a man in China and his concept that I had ripped off Hertz, even though I must be a wizard to be able to change a hard-copy rental form, he could not be answered in the most enlightened sense because his belief did not allow for a more expanded explanation.

Here is how a master thinks. I knew that there were many potential outcomes from that event in my interaction with Hertz. I knew that in one of those parallel theaters Hertz collected their money from my company to the satisfaction of all those participating in that script. I knew that in another parallel theater there was not even an accident in the airport garage, everyone in that theater carried on in a consistent manner supporting that reality, and every possible outcome was available in as many theaters as necessary. These theaters only become as real as they are needed through an observation. This concept of the Many-Worlds Theory holds true for all potentials and only manifest as realities when they are observed by someone.

However, this theory does not excuse one from being responsible for their actions. A person who uses this theory to manifest personal reality has had to overcome doubt and prejudice in order to wield it as a sword of manifestation. A master is beyond right and wrong. They are not moral beings. They are amoral, and that requires a lot of life owned to be able to observe reality in such an unconditional way.

Human beings are always going to observe reality through the neuronets of their culture. There are no great beings that are still influenced by culture. To become great means that you have

31

transcended your culture, the very environment the soul places you in so that you can confront the issues in your life that have yet to be owned. The Asian culture is one that values respect and loyalty. Confrontation is seen as rude and arrogant. Yet these are the very characteristics that must be cultivated in order to become transcendent in that culture. This is why those who are attempting to break out of tradition are usually seen as a threat and subdued by some form of authority. Just look at what the Catholic Church has done to those they called heretics.

"In Tony Busby's *The Bible Fraud*, his history of the life of Jesus is in discord with the accepted religious version. Is it possible that Tony Busby, in his quest to disprove the traditional model of Jesus, shifted into a timeline in which the Jesus he describes in his book is historically accurate according to his own intent? Would this mean that the traditional picture of Jesus as depicted by the Mel Gibson movie, for example, also describes the actual events that occurred on a different timeline? Does the archaeologist's intent create the bones that he or she discovers?"

In these questions we have the answer for the one who poses the question, because each of us is the Observer in any line of questioning and all potentials exist simultaneously. However, they only exist if you can ask the question or contemplate the possibility. Mel Gibson's interpretation is only a reality for those who believe it to be. The Many-Worlds Theory is as big as you can dream it to be.

Archaeologists are Observers in a field of infinite potentials. Those who find the bones are those who expect to find them. Those who do not are also complemented by their Observer in the quantum field. Everyone gets what he or she expects to get in all cases.

Now we can take this concept to another level. You can actually go back in time and plant documents that will appear and test being five hundred years old, and when discovered in three years they will be accepted as a historical text. So technology and those who possess it can create any historical reality or ancient past that they want you to find. It has been suggested that the Nag Hammadi Library was a planted document in just this way. Those documents communicate a much different early Christianity than the Christianity of the New Testament.

It is not so much about what is the truth, because it is all the truth! It just depends on what you want to believe. Quantum reality is going to accommodate those who understand the plasticity of reality and it will accommodate those who insist on living in a linear time reality. The beauty of the quantum field is that everyone gets their conviction.

All we have to do is change our expectations and the elements that make up our environment will change to reflect those changes. If we live in habits and routines, then we will continue to expect the same outcomes on a daily basis. The quantum field simply obeys the orders of each person's thoughts.

There is this story of a traveler who comes to the gates of a village. The elder is sitting there and the traveler asks the elder, "What kinds of people live in this village?"

The elder says, "What kinds lived where you were?"

"Oh, they were terrible. They were selfish. They were greedy."

The elder said, "Well, that is the same kind of people who live here. You had better walk on."

"Since all possible parallel realities are happening simultaneously, is the common denominator of all of them the Observer effect?"

The one piece of information that every human needs to know that will liberate the world is that each person is the Observer in their own life. Whatever they observe, whatever they put their attention on, will be collapsed into personal experience. This is why everyone is responsible for their own reality and no one has the right to blame or to judge anyone or anything else for their condition in life.

Remember the image of the wizard who is walking across

the abyss? As each step is taken, a step materializes under the foot and continues until the crossing is made. This is how reality is formed. Out of thought, the material world manifests.

In this theory of the many worlds, there is a reality in which each of us can heal with a touch, change the past, and know the future. When a student finally says, "Whatever it takes, I am going to accomplish this task," it is this absolute declaration that can seamlessly move us into those new realities. Each of us hesitates to cross that line because we cannot predict the outcome or the impact of that new circumstance in our existing reality.

Evolution on Broadway! I am sure this is the way it works and it has been validated, although controversially, by the Wheeler-Everett model. The implications of this model are so outside of the conventional box of reality that it holds the key to a new paradigm, a paradigm that I would think is already adopted by advanced civilizations. Imagine for a moment that you have adopted this theory. It would automatically render you the experience of ultimate power and responsibility. You would never be a victim. You would only see that at times you make poor choices. Instead of blaming someone else, you would view those choices as the tools you used for navigating on a path toward a specific experience. In the theater of your own mini-world, you have the stage that allows you to experiment with choices and make changes based on those choices. This method of learning would be the most elegant path to achieving your desired experiences.

The drawback to this theory is that some individuals will use it to justify their unscrupulous behavior. They will say that whatever they do does not matter because it isn't really affecting anyone else. They will say that their actions are simply affecting holograms that represent various aspects of themselves. Though this is true, that kind of behavior is not evolutionary. Evolutionary behavior with this model and in real terms is to treat everyone else as you would treat yourself, for that is exactly what you are doing. Self-love is the highest form of love, and this level of knowledge will be reflected in every aspect of your environment. The moment you are no longer emotionally affected by the people, places, things, times, and events of your theatrical production, you have owned the human drama. Now you are an evolutionary being who has earned the right to join a greater community.

"Why is this experience referred to as the illusion? How should we view the world? Is it out there or in here?"

It is called an illusion because it can be dreamed away. Everything exists as a result of a dream or contemplation. Everything can be replaced and changed by a new dream. If quantum mechanics is correct, then we as Observers create our worlds through our own thought. Therefore the world is a construct of our individual beliefs. It is both out there and within. However, we can change the environment and those in it by changing it from within. That is why it is called an illusion. I have heard Ramtha say that everyone is right because they perceive their beliefs played out on the stage of life. It is consistent. Everything and everyone in our life are products of our mind. We are convinced that this reality is shared by everyone else in our life. It appears that way because it is the within that creates the without.

Many years ago there was a doctor in Hawaii who was given the opportunity to work with the criminally insane. He accepted the position with the following criteria. He wanted his own office, access to the files of the patients, but he would never have to come in contact with them. The hospital staff had a high turnover rate because the environment was so dangerous. This doctor read each patient's file. He then went within himself and asked to heal that aspect of himself that was being reflected by the patients in this institution. In a short period of time, patients were reduced in medication, some were released, and the staff reduced because fewer were needed to administer to the needs of the patients. This enlightened doctor knew that everything in his environment was a reflection of his own mind. He healed his environment and everyone in it when he healed those aspects of himself. This theory is radically different from the popular perception that we live at the effect of the environment while being continuously victimized by those circumstances.

"Can we use this theory to explain the conflict as to whether we have only one lifetime or can we experience more than one at a time?"

If we can remember that if a question can be posed, it is already possible. So we can do both, return to this singular lifetime or we can experience more than one lifetime. It is a matter of knowledge and where we place our attention. If you know that you can experience simultaneous, multiple lifetimes, then you are going to have experiences that correlate to that reality. In our school we call that type of experience a "bleed-through" from another time or a parallel time.

Until we own the experiences of the human drama, we will continue to return here to complete this journey. We are frequency specific to the Earth and its opportunities and challenges. We cannot make choices any greater than could the hobbits in the Shire. The hobbits were afraid to venture too far from the comfort of their home because it was the only home they had ever known. Unfortunately, the Earth has to bear the burden of this overpopulated environment. In its own self-defense, the Earth is reacting in violent ways to rid itself of the parasites on its skin, those who do not respect nature and its laws.

Each of us is simply reading off a script and those in our life are mirrors of our mind. Suppose you have a five-year-old son and you see that he already lacks confidence and self-esteem. If every person, place, thing, time, and event comes out of our mind, then we can change our world by changing our own mind. If you can allow your child to be exactly the way he is, then you will have communicated to him that he is loved unconditionally. More importantly, you will not see him as lacking confidence or having low self-esteem, for those are conclusions. Rather you will see him as expressing the attitudes that are necessary for him to own and evolve. These attitudes now become the blessings of his evolution.

If we see our children as evolutionary beings, we will gain the patience and the tolerance for ourselves to allow them to change in their own time. In the process we will have owned our own need for them to be something that they are yet to be. Changing ourself is the secret to changing our world.

The following is a wonderful example of how posing a question has the answer in the question itself.

"If every event comes right out of your head, then you are the only one in the room. If I meet you, did you come out of my head? Do you exist apart from my reality? How are all of these realities butted up against each other?"

The beauty of these questions is that they are exactly as they have been stated. These questions were answered by everything that was asked. You are the only one in the room and that does not correlate with our experience since we appear to interact with other people. But everything comes out of our mind and in a way that makes sense with our perceived reality. I exist apart from your reality but much differently than you perceive me. I can only be in your reality in the way that I make sense to you. None of these realities are butted up against each other because you only need to make sense of the one in which you are consciously aware. Again there is an infinite row of theatrical performances that are simultaneously being produced. You are in one of those theaters. You move to another theater when you change your mind or the way you think, which is saying the same thing.

The reason we can only experience what is frequency specific to us is because that is how we have dreamed it into being. Everything in our tactile environment is the product of our thought. We are frequency specific to everything in it. How many frequency specific realities are there? Well, how many snowflakes have fallen since the beginning of time? Each snowflake has no duplicate. The greatest aspect of this theory and its benefit to you and me is that the theater only plays the show that you have produced. If you change the screenplay, the show changes. If you rewrite the lines for any character, they react to you differently. What aspect of your life do you not ultimately control? It is the illusion that we are separate from the other players in our life that keeps us in a predictable box, and that whole illusion is held together because we believe that what we perceive in our environment is more real than what we can dream internally. As long as humanity believes this, we are easily influenced by corporations, religious dogma, and charismatic leaders.

The purposeful good of these chaotic times is that people begin to question the validity of organized religions that have not provided answers to basic questions. If all they can say is that it is the will of God, then intelligent people will find those explanations to be shallow and will begin to look for more rational understandings. These are not times of peace. They are times of turbulence, and people always ask questions during chaos. These are times similar to those times in the life of the Ram. These times are ripe for truth and ripe for change. Students in the school use these chaotic times to polish and redefine themselves in becoming greater. The advantage of adversity is that it always provides an opportunity to reinvent yourself as greater than the adversity. This is called evolution.

"Reality is always as great
as the question we can ask."

JZ Knight

Chapter 4

Karma and Culture

There is a misconception that we pick our parents. This is an example of a scrap of knowledge that is expanded and accepted as an axiom of truth. The soul has the responsibility for evaluating our evolution, recording our experiences, and designing the set of encoded genetics for our next incarnation. Therefore in our next incarnation, rather than picking our parents we pick a genetic line, and the genetics is often associated with a culture into which we are born.

The genetics give rise to specific propensities in human behaviors. From an evolutionary point of view, these behaviors that feel so "right" are the exact behaviors necessary to overcome in order to evolve on the true spiritual journey. There are no laws that everyone must follow. In fact, each of us is genetically prepared for evolution. We are wearing our journey.

What we refuse to own each lifetime is carried forward as a genetic propensity to the next incarnation. Behaviors that were not owned as wisdom, such as lack, self-pity, fear, or any other limited emotion, will be genetically designed into the next body. The body that we currently inhabit represents the path that needs to be owned. Are we competitive because we are bored or insecure? Are we quick to react? Are we afraid to react? All of these automatic behaviors, unless owned, will find themselves in the genetics of the next body. This is the wisdom and the justice of the soul.

Attitudes, those genetic propensities, can undermine a project's success. Many years ago I had the opportunity to work as an editor for a publishing company. Friends of mine owned the publishing company and we were going to work with a celebrated photographer to produce a photo journal of Ramtha's teachings. This book was going to include the first published photos of Ramtha. Everyone involved in the project were students in the Ramtha teachings.

After several months of progress, the issue of ownership developed. Did this celebrated photojournalist own the pictures or did the organization that gave the photographer permission to take the photographs own the pictures? It took eighteen months to resolve this issue because everyone was defending their position. Once the issue was resolved, the book was completed within six weeks. The delay in the completion of the book had an insurmountable repercussion on the marketing strategy. The attitudes of those involved, compelled to make their point, were the determinate factor in the lack of success for this project.

In another example I had helped my partner pay off a piece of property with money that I had remaining from a small inheritance. This money was another manifestation. The will stipulated that I had to wait ten years before drawing a portion of the money and ten additional years to get it all. But through the focused disciplines learned at the school, I was able to interrupt that legality and receive all of the money within a few years.

When the partnership was over, we put the property on the market for sale. It was an ideal piece of property located on six acres leading to the edge of a pristine, private lake. The well had been drilled and the water was deep, fresh, and fast-flowing. Electrical power was brought to the property and a newly constructed 12' x 20' outbuilding was ready for occupancy. All of the initial costs for preparing the property for financing had been completed. We had every expectation that it would sell within a few months.

The invisible factor that made this ideal property so difficult to sell was our relationship and its unresolved resentments. It was the need on both of our parts to be right. The need to be right is a heavy propensity based on genetics. I focused on this property for six years without a single offer being made on it. It was placed with a real estate agency to see if they could move it. They rarely showed this property to prospective buyers. It was as if they had an unconscious bias against selling it. It was, in fact, consciousness and energy at work. The selling of this property was not about the property but the two partners involved in the property and the opportunity to own aspects of our own personalities.

When we realized that the whole relationship was the responsibility of each of us and blame could no longer be a part of this equation, we began to work together to sell the property. We were talking to each other for the first time in six years. During this period of cooperation I attended an advanced event at our school. During this event each student stayed in a tent. At this event we were taught a new discipline of manifestation. It required a candle and a mirror. That night I focused on a card that represented the sale of the property. I had drawn a lake with a single evergreen tree on the card. In addition, I drew a table with three boxes. One box contained money from the sale, the second box represented a project that I wanted to start, and the third box represented an unknown surprise.

I focused one hour on this card, utilizing the new discipline. I went to sleep after this focus and in the morning we were instructed to go to the "Great Hall" to resume our classes. When I went to the place where I sat at that event, there was a note on my cushion. It simply said, "Is your property still for sale?" It had the name of the person and their phone number. The event was over that afternoon, and within ten minutes of talking to this person we had agreed upon a price. The sale of the property closed in three days and my ex-partner and I had our money.

The property had sold in twenty-four hours, and I was able to use the money to begin a project I had wanted to do for several years. The third box manifested as an unexpected eleven-week paid vacation, and I used this time to begin the new project.

This reality manifested in a way that I could not have predicted, and the third box that represented the gift of time was more valuable than I have words to describe. It allowed me to realize that once again what undermines manifestations must be resolved before the manifestation is free and unencumbered to be realized.

One of the greatest deterrents to creating fabulous realities is culture. I have seen the vast differences in culture as I have presented this material to the various students around the world. Culture creates a specific environment that each of us must overcome in order to own certain aspects of our behaviors. When one becomes aware that they are genetically wearing their journey, then they have an insight into what needs to be changed or owned in order to evolve. This conscious owning is the true spiritual journey, to make known the unknown.

When I tell my story about the rental car at Hertz, it is received differently in different cultures. A man from China, after hearing the story, remarked that I must certainly be a wizard but I still ripped off Hertz. The action of changing the past at the expense of Hertz was morally offensive to him. When the story is told in Italy, I get a standing ovation and they beg me to tell them how to do it. They are not interested in whether anyone got ripped off. They only want to know how to do it for themselves. The remarkable aspect about these two opposing reactions is that both groups can readily justify their reaction because of their allegiance to their culture.

While in Turkey in May 2004, I discovered another remarkable cultural bias. While presenting a two-day workshop during the five days of our stay, our hostess informed us that we were not allowed to pay for anything, including meals, taxis, or even tickets for touring Topkapi Palace in Istanbul. After the third day I asked our hostess, with whom the three of us had become great friends, if she would grant me one favor. Before I told her what it was, she said, "Yes." I asked her if she would kiss me. In her stunned hesitation, like a deer caught in an approaching car's headlights, I asked her if I could pay for lunch. She immediately said, "NO," and reminded me once again that while I was in Turkey, I was her guest. Even though I was joking about the kiss, I had a hunch that buying lunch for her would be more difficult than the other option.

In 1999, on our first trip to Japan to present these teachings, we learned the importance of color. Not only is Japan the land of a thousand bows, it is highly formal and extremely tidy. When you enter a hotel, you exchange your shoes for proper slippers. If you have your own slippers, the hotel manager must examine them to pass the test of managerial scrutiny. When you enter the bathroom in your hotel room, you exchange your room slippers for the bathroom slippers, always a different and obvious color so as not to get the two confused. One of the American staff traveling with us went to the hotel restaurant in his "bathroom" slippers, which were bright green. With the reaction we got from the local Japanese eating in the restaurant, you would have thought a piece of excrement was hanging off the back of one of his slippers. They actually stopped eating and stopped chewing their food. This stunned them. To us they were bright green slippers, simply a different color from those worn by the majority of those in the restaurant.

All of us must overcome our cultural influences to become great beings. Imagine what Buddha had to overcome to become a legendary being. He was born into a royal family as Prince Siddhartha. He married at any early age and became a father with a son. Prince Siddhartha had to break with all tradition. He left his royal duties as next in line for the throne and he left his wife and son to pursue another path. This change in behavior was an agonizing decision, as he went against everything he had been taught and everything that seemed proper within his culture. The result of this break in culture led him to become a legendary being. In order to become something other than a normal human being, we must break with tradition and culture, the very behaviors that seem so "right" in our daily experience.

When I am in Japan, the behaviors of the students are very different from those in Italy or Latin America. The Japanese are duly respectful, tidy, and punctual. About day five of the Retreat, I tell them in a serious voice that they are becoming disrespectful, messy, and tardy to class. After a long pause I tell them, "And I appreciate that." They are learning to become something different than what binds them genetically.

To break with culture and the traditions of culture is the very act of becoming no longer constrained by those values. We are now overcoming our compelling propensity to behave in certain ways. We are overriding the agenda of the soul. We are evolving on the true spiritual journey.

Think of how strong and convincing some of the cultural environments are that continue to hold women as less than equal to men. Where are the men of the Middle East going to go in their next life? They will simply incarnate back as women in the very culture in which inequality is prevalent. What of the men in India who kill their wives because the dowry has run out? Because of their ignorance and what is culturally accepted, what hell will they be born back into? This is the wisdom of the soul in creating genetic bodies for evolutionary purposes. The soul and its system of genetic design is the greatest justice system ever created.

Hindus protect the sacred cow in India because they believe that their parents and grandparents can reincarnate back as a cow. As Ramtha has said to his students, if that is the best that a reincarnation can provide for an evolutionary soul, then why not barbecue them, put them out of their misery, and feed the starving grandchildren. That seems like a much more noble and fulfilling act than having to feed the cows at the expense of being able to feed your family. How much ignorance can be integrated in one day?

"Reality is only as valid as its last observation."

Larry Farwell
Harvard-trained physicist

Chapter 5

Analogical Mind

My favorite experiment that illustrates intent over the environment was done with day-old baby chicks and day-old baby rabbits.

"What is the process that allows day-old baby chicks to have such a profound effect on a machine that is dressed up as a big chicken?"

They were expressing pure intent. The day-old chicks had only one thought and that was getting the attention of mama, that machine, to assist them with their needs such as food, warmth, and protection. They became analogical (one-minded) with their intent, and that is where the power lies.

Masters don't sit down, put on their blinders, and make the sign of the triad to begin the process of creating reality. They have developed this state of analogical mind, and whatever they become is the reality that unfolds. I once saw Ramtha blow in his hand while walking and produce a pearl that he gave to a lady in his audience. We didn't have to wait for him to sit down, put his hands in the C&E® position and make the triad. By then the audience would have left and he would have exhausted the time he could stay in the body. This state of mind is the template for creation. A master is one who has an automatic program for this state of consciousness. Therefore reality is instantaneous with the thought. Students in the school are developing this neuronet of analogical mind. Once it is developed, then one's thought becomes the next reality.

This is why Ramtha says that every time we do a discipline, even if we are not entirely successful with that discipline, we are developing the skill of becoming analogical mind that will eventually allow for its successful accomplishment.

The continual progress in developing analogical mind is what inspires us to continue with the work. One fine day this state of mind will be fully developed. It is in this state of analogical mind that the key to the kingdom of heaven resides, for whatsoever we think in this state of mind readily becomes its reality.

"Can anything happen to someone that has not consciously or unconsciously been created? What part does luck play if we are the creators of our own realities?"

Let's start with luck. Whether it is defined as good or bad, it is generally seen as something that happens without understanding how it happens. We know from ancient wisdom and quantum physics that there is always a cause behind all circumstances. The reason we are considered divine is that our thoughts have an effect on our reality.

No one experiences anything that has not first been contemplated. The biggest obstacle to this understanding is that most of those thoughts are unconscious. They are programs in the brain that are alive and well, yet below the level of normal awareness. These thoughts have been with the brain so long that they are not perceived as active thought patterns and yet reality keeps giving us the feedback that these programs are fully functional.

When students in our school continue to keep creating the same circumstances in their lives, they have learned how to pay attention to their thoughts to understand why this continues. Now they have a choice to make. They can continue with this reality or they can change their thoughts in relation to this and create a different reality

I knew of someone who came home every night after a long day at work and would fall asleep watching the news. The news is rarely uplifting. It boasts of spectacular stories and sensational events, e.g., fires, gun battles, and fatal car accidents. This is probably the worst environment in which to fall asleep because the subconscious is vulnerable when brain-wave activity slows down and you find yourself between states of wakefulness and sleep. Within six months of coming home and falling asleep in front of the television watching the late-night news, this person was hit head-on by a drunk driver. I would venture to guess that this person had seen lots of these kinds of news stories over that previous six-month period. No matter what happens to us, we can always find the contemplations or thoughts that contributed to the experience.

The victims of the world will always point to something outside themselves as the source of what affected them. Was it the drunk driver or was the drunk driver the necessary player to create the eventual outcome? This is examining the experience with a high level of responsibility. Again, what makes us divine is our ability to have thoughts and to suffer the consequences or to celebrate the consequences of those thoughts. We are always in the seat of power.

The more we contemplate something, the more we prepare the soil of our brain to germinate those thoughts into our own experience. We learn in this school exactly how to do this.

"How can something shocking happen to someone who is unaware of having created it?"

It almost always happens on levels of which you are not aware. If you were aware of it you would not continue the thoughts or attitudes that lead to that eventual manifestation. If you make it a habit to sit and watch the news each evening, you are programming realities that increase in probability the more you watch them. If consciousness and energy creates the nature of reality, then what is it that I continue to think about that is going to show up in my life?

The reason there is such a high percentage of teenagers who get their drivers' licenses is because that potential is constantly on their minds for several years before taking the tests. It is a highly expected reality and few things can distract a teenager from that eventual accomplishment. It is the same with day-old baby chicks having the power and single-minded focus to influence a machine to move in their direction. The secret to having what we want or having any experience is demonstrated best with teenagers wanting to drive and with day-old baby chicks wanting to get their mom's attention. The closer we can learn to emulate those levels of intent, the easier it is to manifest our dreams into manifested reality.

"When we analogically tap into the consciousness of another lifeform, are we subject to the conditions of that lifeform? In other words, if I tapped into a dying tree, does that mean that I will also die a little? What if I tapped into the consciousness of another being from another reality?"

There is a concept in physics called entanglement. It states that once we have an interaction with something, we are forever affected by it. So you may become aware of certain conditions but you would not need to adopt those conditions. It is information you would be receiving. You could know the thoughts of a tree. I understand the concept of long thought because I did become analogical with a tree with the intent to know its mind.

Ramtha taught us in his classes on Dimensional Mind how to become analogical with something in nature in order to know its mind. These initiations were called pagan dances. We spent the day making a mask that depicted the concept in nature that we wanted to understand. As we danced and focused on our mask, we became the concept. In that process we understood the mind of that concept in nature. There is a great tree in Yosemite National Park called the General. It is 20,000 years old. Imagine what you would know if you became analogical with its mind.

You can know the mind of anything or anyone if you become analogical with it, even about another being in another reality. We have a part of our brain called the lower cerebellum that is hooked up to the quantum field or what Ramtha calls the mind of God. Anything that has lived has contributed its wisdom to the mind of God, and that is why we can know anything with which we become analogical.

The concept of using focus to become anything follows an exact formula. It is simple in concept, but more difficult in application. In essence you must become what it is you want to experience. The specific techniques are taught at the school.

This seems simple but it is a challenge by the very nature of most human Observers. Until we are trained to hold our focus to the exclusion of everything else, including the demands of the body, we will not be successful initiating a new dream. Human beings lose concentration six to ten times each minute. Everyone has "adult deficit disorder (ADD)." In school we learn how to hold a concentrated focus even in simulated hostile environments. This training is imperative for the human Observer to be successful.

The pagans knew how to become what it was they wanted to experience. They used the "pagan" holidays for their festivals and dances. They would put on a mask that emulated the concept that they wanted to know and experience. During their dances they would go into a trance state and have an experience of the mind of that concept. We did this at our school in what were called trainings in Dimensional Mind. I became a tree in one of my dances with a mask made from a tree, and during the dance I understood the mind of a tree. I understood its long thought and absolute patience in living. I remembered Ramtha's question: What does a tree know that you do not know? I remembered Ramtha's answer: The tree does not know how to die; only humans know how to do that. These concepts in nature I could have never understood as a human being, as they were foreign to my own personality.

Since that day I have had a deepening appreciation and

greater understanding for trees. I still have a dream to buy the trees on lands where some people have to cut them down to pay the land taxes. Land taxes continuously increase and become a hardship for those on fixed incomes. I would buy the trees, pay the taxes, and put a moratorium on the cutting of the trees. This idea came after my dance in which I understood the wisdom and the majesty of trees.

Ramtha tells the story of the witch doctor who puts on the animal skin and rubs his body with the blood of the buffalo so that during the dance, when the witch doctor reaches a heightened state of trance, he can see where the buffalo are grazing. In the morning the tribe would set out for its hunt. That is concentrated focus using the formula to become what it is you want to experience or know.

"Given that above example, do we know more than we remember?"

Of course we know more than we can remember. We are called the forgotten Gods. We have forgotten the knowledge and the experience of the four great questions: Who are we? Where did we come from? What is our destiny? How do we fulfill that destiny? That is what we have forgotten. There is no religion or mainstream philosophy that has adequately answered those questions, and yet they are answered brilliantly in the first days of the Beginning Retreat.

Intuition is a common name for accessing that part of the brain (the midbrain) that has access to the past, the future, and remote locations. It knows more than what is stored in the neocortex. If we learn to access this part of our brain, then we can see the timeline of our most probable future and make choices based on what we see. That is how I survived the train crash on its way to Varanasi. We can know what another person is thinking or what is contained in a box at a location many miles away. We can access a past event, and if we still suffer the consequences of that event we can change its current effect on our life. This part of the brain does not comply with the rules of linear time, which gives the midbrain its quantum characteristic of being able to access all times simultaneously.

However, the midbrain is not our greatest asset in remembering. Remembrance is a function of our neocortex, and that organ is relegated to this lifetime. Our neocortex is indigenous to this body and would not have the information of a past-life experience. That is why I find it somewhat suspicious that so many people do past-life readings. All past lives would be recorded in the soul and in the electromagnetic bands that surround our body. This information of the past can be accessed in the quantum field through the lower cerebellum and is a function of an analogical desire. You can know anything; however, to do so you must learn how to package and present a question properly to the part of the brain that has access to the information you want to know. This is exactly the method Einstein used to learn about the mysteries of light, its absolute speed, gravitation, and the special theory of relativity. He could not have known that with the information that was currently available at the time of his curiosity. He received the visions of his contemplations through the lower cerebellum and later translated those into mathematical equations. That is how you can know anything.

We can determine when we are in a trance state that is necessary to create a new dream. When you are no longer concerned with the environment, your body, or time, you are in the present moment. We call that a trance state. It means that consciousness has moved into a deeper level of mind. It is this level of mind that can take an idea and observe it into your life. That is what we learn to do at our school. It is a skill that can be developed. It is also called concentrated focus on a single idea. This is the secret to manifesting anything you want into your life. You must move beyond the distractions of your environment, your body, and time to accomplish this concentrated state. You will know you are in the proper state of mind if your internal picture of what you are focusing on is more real than the external environment. Driving down the highway and missing your exit is an example of an internal process that is more real than the external environment.

"Is there a method of repatterning a negative response in the body brought on by a negative thought or memory?"

If you can remember the original incident and view it in a detached manner, then you bypass the predictable response and its associated emotions. This skill is called observation. This is the only way in which you can heal a troubled incident and its emotions. If, however, you remember that incident to the point where the emotions associated with the incident are experienced again, then you will have reinforced the neurological connections so that this incident and its emotions can easily occur again and again.

The only successful way to retire memories or circumstances from your past in which you still suffer is to observe them into retirement. Observation, without engaging the incident that results in the chemistry of emotions, will atrophy those connections in the brain. Without those connections, there is no program to create the thought that creates the emotions. This action of observation is an important aspect of the true spiritual journey.

"A rich man is one who has enough."

Chinese Proverb

Chapter 6

PERSONAL LIFE

I never want to see any of the questions that are sent into the program before they are read on the air. This gives the answer a fresh and unrehearsed response. Here is one that required an unrehearsed answer.

"As a frontman for RSE, one who is seen as a wise and knowledgeable being, having the power to then instruct others in the art of unfolding the unlimited that lies within those who come and pay money to learn about themselves, I must ask you what it is that you bring to the table, as it were, to be reflected back to the individual and the group as a whole? Also, explain the benevolence of defeat, disappointment, worry, and strife in a student's life."

That is an excellent and fair question. The first quality that is reflected back to the students is my unwavering enthusiasm for this work. Enthusiasm is a result of having knowledge and an application to experience that knowledge that adds to the quality of my life on a consistent basis. This leads to change and change leads to evolution, the purpose of life. In addition, I have been a student for nearly twenty-five years in a school that is anything but easy. The experiences that I have had and that I have witnessed with others are a source of inspiration to those wanting to know themselves and the power that lies within. My experiences as a student are told as stories of illustration during the Beginning Retreats and in this book. They are always told as an example of what can be done by anyone who applies this knowledge. The examples always point to the greatness in all people.

As a teacher in the school, I have seen the miracles in our school and the miracles in every part of the world. Each of these experiences reinforces my own truth, and I have expectancy at every event that these miracles will continue and increase. That is exactly what seems to be happening. When there is an Observer who views reality through this neuronet of high expectancy, then reality unfolds accordingly, and this is what I bring to the table at every event.

The benevolence of defeat, disappointment, worry, and strife is in the understanding that these are interpretations of an experience. One person's worry is another person's fascination. The other important aspect of this kind of feedback is to understand that consciousness and energy creates the nature of reality. If one's reality is filled with these kinds of experiences, then one must go back and examine the thoughts and attitudes that led to these realities. With examination comes clarity, and with clarity comes the opportunity to choose to change. That is a benevolent system.

"I don't even know what consciousness is. I'd like someone to define consciousness."

Consciousness is the river of all thought. We use that river from which to select a thought. With this thought, we have learned how to create mind through concentrated focus. And mind is the template by which our world is organized.

"So then, perhaps, without application of concentrated focus, the template by which our world is organized is genetically and environmentally determined...?"

That is exactly right. Without knowledge we are left with

the battle of mass-to-mass survival.

"Is there a formula for enlightenment down to twenty years or less, because some of us are running on bald tires?"

First of all, it is not my formula. I am a student applying this formula. But I can tell you something that should give you hope. The students who come to school now for their eight-day Beginner's Retreat accomplish in that week what is equivalent to what the advanced students accomplished in fifteen years.

In other words, there is a level of accomplishment that is readily accepted by the new students that allows them this extraordinary speed in accomplishing the disciplines that lead to mastery and enlightenment. As a beginning student, if you knew that the advanced students were mastering the disciplines of levitation and invisibility, wouldn't you be able to more readily accept the concept that you could find an index card with a picture on it that you drew, even if you were blindfolded in a field the size of two football fields? Beginning students readily find their cards in this discipline. When the advanced students first learned this discipline, we shouted with joy when we found the fence. The level of acceptance for finding your card on that large field has greatly increased since those first days more than a decade ago. As a recent example, I presented a two-day workshop in Austria with 107 students new to this work. Those students found fifty cards in fifty minutes. So bald tires or not, there is always time to become a master in this work. The moment you decide to dedicate your life to becoming something greater than you have been, time will accommodate your desire and nothing can interrupt that destiny unless you change your mind. You are always in control of your destiny by how you think. The Observer, as the great sun looking through the stained-glass window of that majestic cathedral, will give you anything that you hold as a priority of mind. It has no prejudice as to whether that is decay or eternity.

Just after Kenny Thompson, whom Ramtha calls Master of the Cards, began to demonstrate his ability to see through matter, I was often asked by students around the world, "How long did it take him to see through the cards?" He has said that it took about three weeks from the moment he dedicated himself to this preferred discipline. I have told students that it was the moment he made up his mind that he was going to master this discipline no matter how long it took. It was his attitude of whatever it takes and no matter how long it takes that allowed this to happen in an incredibly short amount of time. If you can get this understanding, then you will know the secret to instant or quick manifestations. Subconscious mind responds to a neuronet, and a collection of neuronets becomes an attitude. If the attitude is whatever it takes and however long it takes, that is the same as looking into the future and seeing that it is inevitable. Inevitability is the same as now to the subconscious mind. So it is not about doing the disciplines every day for the sake of doing them every day. We do the disciplines every day because they are a natural part of whatever it takes, and that is not a hardship. It is simply the way that it is. That statement of absolution is what allows the Observer to look through a neuronet that will accept nothing less than its desire. That formula holds true for every one of us. When Ramtha says that "God is decision," this is an example of that very concept. Attitude is everything! You are only as old or running on bald tires as you perceive yourselves to be.

On his birthday in July, I took my eighteen-year-old son out for lunch at a popular restaurant. He ordered a Coke and I ordered a tall microbrew beer. The waiter said to me, "Could I see some ID?" His nametag said Amit, so I assumed he was from India and under strict orders about the consequences of serving minors.

My son is laughing uncontrollably while I produce my driver's license. Amit looks at the license and says "Whoo." He sees that I am 58 years old. Because I am no longer a minor he gives me back my license and brings me my beer. My son and I laugh for the next ten minutes until we are brought our food. Whether the waiter was overcautious or I looked extra fabulous that day, it was a reminder that we are only as old as we perceive ourselves to be.

I made some comments about investments in one of the programs, and here is a question that resulted from those comments.

"What is your opinion of gold and its use to build toward sovereignty?"

Gold is a fabulous investment for many reasons. I remember Ramtha telling his students to buy five ounces of gold. He told us that this gold would be used to pay for any increase in taxes that might be levied against our properties. A person would need to be holding a lot of gold to pay off a standard mortgage, but you would be able to use it to make payments when the dollar becomes worthless.

Gold is purchased as a hedge against falling currencies, political instability, and war. The U.S. dollar is headed to the basement, as all of these conditions have unfolded. Gold and the U.S. dollar have an inverse relationship to each other. As one falls, the other climbs. I would suggest that you buy gold and silver currency as well as precious metal stocks. I would not suggest that you leverage your buys using margin accounts, as they are risky if there is a sell-off and you are unprepared. You should also remember that if you buy stocks, you will pay a tax on any profits. It is much more private to sell your gold and silver to a discrete coin dealer.

Silver is currently undervalued. It is generally valued at one-tenth or one-fifteenth of the value of gold. If it reaches its normal value ratio again, it will instantly triple its already increasing value. Everyone can afford to purchase one-ounce silver coins. When China upgrades its citizens into a convenience society, the demand for silver will be exponentially greater than what can be produced. Silver is used for computers and modern appliances. Imagine what the demand for silver will be when the Chinese create a middle class.

However, here is a caution that has historical relevance. If there is a rumor or a statement from the government that gold or silver might be recalled, as it was in the 1930s, then you should convert all of your gold and silver currency into numismatic coins. In 1933 gold was valued at $4.00 an ounce. The U.S. government recalled all of the gold and was willing to pay $8.00 an ounce for it. Everyone had a year to trade in their gold for a quick one hundred percent profit. Anyone caught with gold was sentenced to prison. At the end of the year when all of the gold had been recovered, gold was declared to be worth $32.00 an ounce and was used to pay against the U.S. debt. We are in a similar sitation today. Numismatic coins, antique jewelry, and dental gold were the only gold items not subject to the recall.

There is no other appreciating commodity, with the possible exception of oil, that will stand the test of time as will gold and silver. I heard Ramtha say that gold would climb to $2,000.00 an ounce. Other experts are conservatively estimating that gold will climb to $1,650.00 an ounce. Once gold hits these appreciated values, it would be a good time to sell the currency and use the profits to pay against any mortgage that is remaining. In times of severe crisis you cannot eat gold but you can eat the foods that you will grow and raise on a sovereign property.

On a more personal note, I have been asked if I am in a relationship that is better than average and if I have my domestic life together. At the time of this question I had a family that included two children living at home, a wife, a dog, a lot of fish, squirrels and birds that we fed, and a flock of chickens. Those are the domestic aspects of our family. For the past eight years I have been away from my family and out of the country on an average of two weeks each month. What has allowed me to continue this schedule is that I have my personal life together.

My own personal happiness would never last if it depended on anything or anyone outside of myself. Happiness is always the result of self discovery through having new experiences. The antithesis of happiness will be the result of routine.

In my experience, marriage and its success is directly proportional to the amount of freedom that exists within that marriage. In other words, if both partners are free to explore and discover what interests them, then there is always a freshness and renewal that exists. If the purpose of the relationship is bigger and more expansive than the needs of either individual, then what occurs is an adventure that is all-pervasive that sustains and transcends the pettiness that often plagues a relationship.

The greatest passion you will feel for your partner is the discovery and fascination of their mind. If you do not find each other's mind stimulating, you will grow tired of the repetitious behavior. If you are in a continual mode of learning, you will be of utmost interest to your partner. If you are a dreamer who can dream new dreams, your conversations will be stimulating and contagious. But the moment routine becomes a predominant part of the relationship, you will either begin to erode the passion that exits between you and your partner or you will find a new avenue of interest.

"In researching the Ramtha material on Earth changes, I am both frightened and depressed. There are some very bleak timelines for humanity."

That is true. They are already prevalent, but they are not bleak for all of humanity. Here is what Ramtha has been telling his students for a quarter of a century. The potential for economic collapse is a strong potential and more likely now than in the past with the U.S. trade deficit and the Middle East countries thinking of selling their oil in exchange for the euro rather than the U.S. dollar. I am almost certain that this is why Saddam Hussein was taken down. He was starting to favor the euro over the U.S. dollar as an exchange for oil, and this could not be tolerated by the U.S. and its fragile currency. The same story is developing in Iran. In addition, the Earth is suffering from the abuse of its inhabitants. It is being drained of its blood. We call it oil. The waters and the air are polluted to unprecedented levels, and the Arctic is melting at an alarming pace due to global warming. Remember, every organism wants to live and will fight for its survival. You are going to see the Earth increase its efforts to revolt and cleanse itself of its parasites. There is the ever-growing concern about avian flu and the possibility that a global epidemic might develop. You can cite more concerns. There is no shortage of them at this point.

To be prepared for any of these realities is the ultimate love of self and family. To be sovereign, in my opinion, is the quintessential act of spiritual understanding. Being sovereign means that you can provide for your own means, without being dependant on anyone or anything else. This freedom includes a home that is mortgage-free and the necessary resources to continue living for an extended period of time without being able to purchase goods.

We were told to buy a small piece of land, dig a well, and test the water. We were told to plant a garden that both feeds our family and produces extra food at the end of harvest that can be canned and put away for future times. While times are still calm, there are many local highway markets that have fruits and veggies that can supplement or provide for your canning. The suggestion was to buy extra cans of food every time you went to the store and to put that food away. You can rotate the food according to dates if you do this for several years. We were told to buy everything that we would need to maintain our sovereignty in case you could not purchase anything. We were told to save seeds and to learn how to harvest the seeds from our summer gardens. We were told to have the necessary medicines and vitamins for our family. In addition, every family should purchase gold, as its value will soar if the dollar is devalued. The best information is contained on the audio- or videotapes called *Change: The Days to Come*. Ramtha did that teaching in 1986. Some people have criticized him because they have said that his predictions have not manifested. If you get this teaching, you will be amazed at how many, if not all, of his predictions have come true. He has told his students many times that he knew they would be slow to become sovereign, and he delivered that information with that in mind.

When you are a conqueror, you are also a master strategist. I believe Ramtha prepared against all potential outcomes so that no matter what manifested, he was prepared. He has made that same suggestion to his students. Is the scenario we have been talking about going to happen? Probably. Can the scenario be changed? Yes, but if you cannot manifest bread in your hands on command, it would be prudent to buy extra food and have it available until you have perfected the art.

So my suggestion is twofold: First, you want to follow the preparedness suggestions outlined by Ramtha in his 1986 teaching of *Change* and, second, you need to learn how to create reality by affecting the quantum field of all possibilities. If you do these two, then you have prepared yourselves against all future scenarios.

I introduced my son Navarreaux on one of the Webcast programs and I was asked to make a comment about him. I want to give you an idea of the level of mind that the children have that attend our school. Navarreaux came to me yesterday and said, "Dad, what happens when you shoot a laser into a torsion field?" And I said, after an appropriate pause, "Let me get back to you on that." That same day I talked to a scientist in our school and asked him the same question. He said to me, "Let me get back to you on that." What I love the most is that there was a question from one of our five-year-olds for which our physics instructor and I didn't have an immediate answer. That is the level of mind that is being developed in our school for the young children.

Since Ramtha is famous for sending runners, and his model of reality is called the triad, I answered some questions about these two concepts.

The triad is the symbol and template that depicts Ramtha's Model of Science. It answers the most fundamental of questions regarding humanity: Who am I? Where did I come from? What is my destiny? How do I fulfill that destiny? It describes the journey of humanity from the conception of time to the present moment and to the potentials in the future. It is an all-encompassing model of the nature of reality. To get a more detailed explanation, the reader can purchase Ramtha's book, *A Beginner's Guide to Creating Reality*.

Runners are opportunities for experience that are specifically sent by Ramtha to help his students. Ramtha may say that he will send us a runner to help us better understand a concept or that delivers a specific experience. In one of the sessions Ramtha asked his students how many were still addicted to their sexuality. I didn't raise my hand nor did many of the other students. He looked at our group and said, "I will send you a runner so that you have a better understanding of addiction." Several weeks later I had the experience of my own level of sexual addiction, so I got his runner.

In 1982 Ramtha sent me a classic runner before I had even heard his name. At the time I was living just north of San Diego in an elegant beachfront community. It was a Friday evening and a friend of mine was getting ready to drive to my house from San Francisco. She was planning to arrive on Saturday morning about 11:00 a.m., as she was driving straight through the night. Five minutes before she finished packing her car, a stranger ran into her house, put a piece of paper on her dresser, and then ran right back out and disappeared. She looked at the paper and it was a flyer announcing that Ramtha would be in Los Angeles on the following morning at 9:00 a.m. She had never heard the name Ramtha. However, she was fascinated by the unconventional method in which she received the communication and the fact that she would be driving through Los Angeles at 9:00 a.m. the next morning on her way to my house. She was curious and attended the Dialogue that Saturday morning. In those days, at the end of the class the organization would copy the sessions on cassette tapes and sell them to the participants for a nominal fee. She brought me the cassette tape of the Dialogue she had just attended. I listened to the tape that weekend and signed up for the next Dialogue that happened to be in Seattle one month later. This is an example of a literal runner that had been sent by Ramtha to help one of his future students, even though I had yet to hear his name. Other runners may come in the form of newspaper articles, movies, and books that fall off a shelf at the library, and from almost anywhere that delivers a message or experience according to his intent.

To continue my thoughts regarding children in conjunction with what I had recently learned at an event, Ramtha reminded us that children were always building something innovative and new when they played. He said that they never go to their past, that they always build something for the future. In contrast, adults almost always use the past as a reference to build something new. When children reach a certain age, they lose the interest to create new things and begin to maintain an identity of who they are expecting themselves to be. This means that we have stopped dreaming about possibilities. This then begins the aging process through the redundancy of thoughts.

If children can be taught to continue to dream, which is an out-of-time activity, they would not begin to age as quickly as those who stop dreaming. Children are fortified and continuously rejuvenated by their own creative minds. Children do not have a past as long as the future is as bright as building something toward it. So how we get rid of our past is by having a future that is more captivating than the memories of our past.

The greatest era of my life previous to becoming a student in the school was my experience of the 1960s. Ramtha has stated that the greatest cultural revolution in modern times was the sixties. He has dedicated whole evenings to expressing the impact of that group on a global culture. The music of the sixties was written and performed by troubadours of truth that condemned segregation, immoral wars, and the prejudice to equal rights. My timing was perfect to experience this cultural revolution. I was a high school senior in an East Coast Preparatory School when the Beatles first performed on the *Ed Sullivan Show*.

During my November midterm exams in my freshman year of college, and after discovering the temperatures in Alabama were forty degrees higher than in Pennsylvania, I got on a bus sanctioned by the university and rode for thirty hours. Most of the students on the bus were hoping to walk with Dr. Martin Luther King, Jr., in the march to the courthouse in Selma, Alabama. I was looking for warmer weather. When we arrived in Selma, smiling African-Americans took us into a local church after escorting us off the bus. We slept underneath the church pews for safety, as several churches had been bombed in the days previous to our arrival. All night long beautiful black men guarded the church. This was my first encounter witnessing the South and its deep prejudice against black Americans. The next morning before the march we walked to breakfast. We were allowed only to walk as couples rather than in a group that could be easily targeted. It was a surreal environment for a freshman in college with a cloistered view of the real world and its battles.

There was a tremendous march that day in Selma. As we got closer to the courthouse we passed public schools, and the predominately black children came out of the windows and the doors of those schools to join the march. In a few moments the crowd had swelled to an unexpected gathering. It was a happening of megaproportions. There were police everywhere. They were on nervous horses and they were standing in deep rows in front of the courthouse. These police were heavily armed with sticks, helmets, and dogs. The atmosphere was electric with tension that escalated with each step that drew us closer to the courthouse. Somehow that morning march and the speeches on the steps of the courthouse went without major incident. It wasn't until later that it became extremely dangerous.

Several hours after everyone moved away from the courthouse, a group of blacks, white students, and black civil rights leaders met in the middle of a street where many of those who had marched were sitting. Dr. Martin Luther King, Jr., arrived in a pink 1956 Cadillac and talked to the group. He was encouraging his principles of nonviolence against some of the militant blacks who were angry with passive attempts at justice. The militants were arguing that a nonviolent strategy was not getting the message across. Dr. Martin Luther King, Jr., left in his car. At the top of the hill on this same street a police parade of motorcycles was forming and beginning to weave their bikes back and forth. Suddenly and without warning they stormed down the hill right over and through the crowds that were sitting in the street. It happened in an instant, and people were in chaos. The militants began breaking bottles to use as weapons. I instinctively ran to a yard and jumped over a fence. As I anxiously looked under the fence, the owner of the house came from behind me with a large kitchen knife and said to get out of his yard I was now between a knife and a riot just over the fence. I crawled under the fence and in moments the police were gone and the crowds left in disarray and shock.

I made my way to the street corner and walked into a bar. I was welcomed in that bar, as I was recognized as one of the white students from the North who had come to help make a difference in the lives of those who had been severely suppressed. For the next several hours before my bus went back to the university, I drank beer, laughed, enjoyed lively conversation, and I began to appreciate a group of people I hardly knew existed two days prior to this experience. This trip became a turning point in my life. I became active in the antiwar movement when I returned to the university. This sets the stage for the revolution that was beginning to build its momentum, and the music, the antiwar movement, the civil rights movement, and the rights of women were spawned in this culture. I was living in San Francisco and Berkeley in the late sixties. This was an education far beyond what my university could offer. We were living in the midst of change and revolution. It was a dynamic time.

The selective service draft was a frightening reality. Most people knew that if you were drafted, you were going to Vietnam and for many young men that was a "death sentence." I missed eight predraft physicals by moving from state to state. I had been rejected by my local draft board as a "conscientious objector." This was a legal status that allowed one to object to the war on religious or moral reasons. I had been turned down through an application and interview process, and my only viable recourse seemed to be to go to Canada. There were thousands of young men who were going to Canada to avoid the draft.

My father had been an all-American football player from LSU, one of the football powerhouses of the 1940s. He was a lieutenant commander in the merchant marine, the youngest officer to have full responsibility of a ship. I, on the other hand, was taking several years off from college to play music, enjoy the freedom of the sixties movement, and grow my hair down the middle of my back. It was in these circumstances that I called my father and told him that I was intending to do whatever I could to stay out of the draft. I explained to him that the only way I could resubmit my conscientious objector application for review was if one of the members of the local draft board would sign a paper allowing me one more interview. In a surprise answer, he said he would see what he could do. As it turns out, the member of the draft board that he contacted died several weeks later. On top of his desk of stacked papers was the last thing he signed, his approval to review my draft status. It was a kind of karmic payback for my support of the civil rights movement and the resistance to an immoral war. I hired an attorney, and through the legal system I was able to stay out of the draft. At twenty-six years old I was no longer concerned, as no one had been drafted after that age since World War II.

I have always thought that Ramtha had a part in this unfolding drama. I have not talked to him about it, but he has smiled at me often during his talks about the troubadours of truth who created a cultural revolution in the 1960s.

"After the *What the Bleep!?* movie, I am now aware of Ramtha, but in listening to some of the older teachings I have come to realize that I am now in debt, live near the beach, and need some quick advice. Can you help?"

The most important step to take at this point is to learn how to consciously create reality. This will give you the accelerated path to knowledge that will open the doors of opportunity to expedite your new hopes and dreams. With this training, living in the city with a normal debt load will not seem so overwhelming. In addition, what was seductive about the city and its stimulation will lose its glitter, and there will be a natural draw to the learning environment of nature. Once you have a taste for this change of lifestyle, you will have your power intact to create an easy transition.

The cities are the most dangerous places in the world. They are where disease breaks out and water supplies become scarce or polluted. Once you are inside the prison, it is not so easy to get out. Remember what happened during the climatic weather systems of the South in 2004 and 2005. Nobody could get out of town, and those who attempted to leave ran out of gas before they could reach another gas station. Everyone became stranded. Many other people who were trapped in the city became desperate, dangerous, or victims.

The most difficult step to take is the first one. However, from experience of having taken many first steps, it is the only step that opens the door to the next opportunity. Once you have moved through the door, the next door appears. I have never taken more than ten years to pay off any of the houses I have owned. Before understanding how to consciously create reality, I was always on the thirty-year plan.

In 2001 I was obliged to undertake an expensive and highly technical construction project. Without the knowledge of the school I could have easily become paralyzed with the fear of having to do something that I had neither the money, time, or the expertise to do. I made a card with an appropriate symbol, a rainbow, and the words "Project Completion" on it. Blank cards with a drawing on it are used as tools to manifest a specific outcome. I focused on that card once a day for forty days. At the end of the six weeks I had the necessary money, the expertise, and plenty of extra time to do the project. The money came from the aforementioned real estate sale that had been a difficult project for over six years. Within a week of deciding to do the project, I was notified that I was receiving an unexpected eleven-week paid vacation and I was introduced to an associate who had years of experience in the type of project on which I was working. Everything fell into place once the choice was made to take the next step. The most delightful surprise came at the end of eighteen months. On the last day of the project, a rainbow appeared in the north just as the tractor was turned off for the last time. The whole scene was complete, just as my card had been drawn.

"I attended a Beginner's Retreat about one year ago and since then my life has been ripped apart. My finances,

my family, and everything in-between have been affected. It was the greatest experience of my entire life. So what happened?"

You changed, and the people, places, things, times, and events in your world changed to reflect those changes. It sounds harsh, but your new mind has new reflections in the world. The old must fade away for the new to emerge. You are like the phoenix arising from the ashes. Generally when students go home from a Beginning Retreat there is a gradual adjustment to the new changes. In your case, it was more extreme.

You are one of the eighty-four to ninety percent of the students who attend these Retreats that have the greatest week of their life, so far. Obviously, it is going to have an impact on your current life. What I am about to say may not be of consolation, but you have accepted those changes you made during that week and have not let your old personality back to compromise those changes. I had a similar experience. I left a very successful business to move to the Pacific Northwest in order to be near the school. I was a major partner in a start-up company that unexpectedly generated annual sales of fifty-five million dollars several years after I left. When I arrived in Yelm, I had to ask for a five-dollar-an-hour job three times before I was given a chance to prove myself. I never looked back, but it did cross my mind that I might have done it differently by commuting for several years before jumping in with both feet. However, that was just my old personality trying to justify having lost the opportunity to experience an unprecedented annual income. However, in retrospect and given the same opportunity, I would do it the same way again.

Soon after my move to Yelm, my life organized itself into a higher level of mind. The term in biology is called perturbation. Many species when faced with adversity disassemble and reorganize at a higher level of efficiency. The period in-between these states is called chaos.

"How do we build the neuronets to realize the invisible? I am referring this question back to your levitation

experience under the tutelage of Ramtha."

The visible versus the invisible is simply what you have mapped in your brain to see. The eyes see everything but the visual cortex only sees what it has been trained to see. We build neuronets to see the invisible the same way we build neuronets for any experience. First you must have the knowledge mapped in the brain as a potential and then a technique that would give you that exact experience. There is the famous story of the Spanish coming to the shores in the fifteenth or sixteenth century in their massive boats. The indigenous people, who saw the Spanish, saw them as if they were walking on water because they had not been trained to see their boats. This is exactly how we learn to see the invisible. First we get the knowledge, then we practice the training, and then we have the experience. This holds true for any experience, seen or unseen. With my levitation experience, even though my eyes were open the entire time, I did not see anything from the time I lifted off until my second foot hit the ground. Then I could see again. Kenny Thompson, Master of the Cards, sees what is already floating on top of the playing card. It is not that he focuses and the image on the card appears. The image is always floating on the card, and everyone can be trained to develop the skill to see what is always there.

"Often the concept of enlightenment is portrayed as being peaceful and without the need for motivation or purpose. Is there a future beyond enlightenment?"

If that were the definition of enlightenment, there would be no future. This is a misinformed concept. Enlightenment is often associated with a picture of the Buddha sitting under a tree in some form of contemplation, but an enlightened person is extremely busy with their own evolution. A master would never sacrifice his evolution for a life of peace and happiness. A master prefers confrontation, challenge, and adversity. It is these concepts that mold and evolve an individual into a transcendental being.

When I went to India several years ago, I was a guest at the Sri Aurobindo ashram, which was the home of a famous Indian guru. People from all over the world came to listen to his discourses. In a private meeting with him, he was telling me that he had reached a perfect state of peace and happiness. I told him that peace and happiness were not an aim or an intended interest of mine or that of most of the other students in our school. I told him that making known the unknown was our purpose, that it was rarely accompanied by peace or happiness but rather by challenge and adversity. I told him that it was our purpose to conquer ourselves, and that entailed owning aspects of our own fragmented personality that could only respond in limited emotions to the circumstances in our life. I told him that this process of ownership was often very uncomfortable. He looked confused and asked me to continue to explain. I told him that in creating a new reality, when we focused on a manifestation the process was often frustrating but that perseverance with that idea would eventually create its reality. He asked me if I could create something out of nothing. I said that I could. He asked me if I would show him how I did it at our next meeting. I assured him that I would.

I went back to my room that evening and wondered how I was going to create something out of nothing in front of him and everyone else he was going to invite. I was both exhilarated and nervous at the same time. It was one of those defining moments in my life that was going to be profound one way or the other. I tossed and turned all night thinking of what I was going to do. By morning I had came up with a strategy that would eliminate the immediate pressure of performance but might still satisfy the guru and his staff. I came up with the concept that I would manifest rain in three days. This would be a formidable challenge in that the rainy season was over and the prospect of rain in the next several weeks was next to nil. I was confident that I could do it.

As it turned out, the rains came in three days, which was a surprise to many. The rains especially surprised the taxi drivers, who had already disconnected their windshield wipers for the season. They did not expect any rain and they needed those same wires to power the heater. For a few moments I was able to bask in this satisfaction. But as the Ram has told us many times, you are only as successful as your last manifestation, and none of us has yet to earn the right to rest on the laurels of our past. In the next moment we are contemplating another manifestation that allows us to make known the unknown. So enlightenment is not someone who sits behind a serene smile. It is someone who knows that they are God, that their purpose along with every other being is to make known the unknown, and that evolution is always a challenge. As it turned out, the guru died within a year of our visit.

"How can a divorced father create having his children live with him when the mother will not allow that?"

I had a similar situation with my first son. After seven years in a relationship, my seven-year-old son and his mother moved to Southern California. I wanted to raise my son but not with his mother and under those circumstances. After several months he called me and said that he wanted to move back to Washington. I told him to focus on that happening but not to mention that he had talked to me about it. I knew that his mom would only tighten her grip on him if she thought I was suggesting that he move back. I told my son that if he stayed focused on it, she would eventually change her mind. His mother called me several weeks later and said that she was sending him back. We set a date that I would pick him up at the airport. After he moved back, we shared our home together until he moved into his own apartment at eighteen. I had the challenge and the privilege of providing for him all of those years.

The importance of what I am telling you is that children are more powerful in the clarity and desire of their intent than the parents who are simply reacting to the betrayals of the past. If you can get your children to hold a dream in the silence of their thoughts, a parent is powerless against such a pure mind. In addition, when my son's mother decided that she could not hold him in Southern California against his wishes, she felt as if she were accommodating his wishes, not the hopes of his father. Separated partners are vicious when it comes to their children and they will use the children to punish each other.

Until the time comes that your dream is realized, there are things that you can do to accelerate this process. First and foremost, you should not get into continuous debates with your ex-wife. This will only fortify her position and make the issue about you and her, not your children. Secondly, I would suggest that you involve yourself in things that bring you a natural passion for life. Your enthusiasm for life itself will do more to raise the hopes of your children wanting to spend time with you than all the conversations that you could possibly have. Passion for a hobby or a project is infectious in a wonderful way. And, thirdly, you must be patient. If you can continue to enjoy your life while holding the dream on your end, then you will have activated the forces of the unseen to work on your behalf. That is what I did that allowed his mom to suggest that my son come back and live with me.

"I read and hear about many adolescents engaging in destructive behavior. Now that my kids are approaching that stage, am I attracting that for my kids by worrying about it? Am I planting those potentials in their consciousness by warning them? Can I not focus on it and therefore it will not be a part of their reality?"

You are not attracting anything into your children's lives by your own fear. You are attracting it into your own life, and your children are the reflections of those fears. Your children have a multitude of ways to reflect back to you your own attitudes. We must remember that there is no one outside of our own mind, only reflections of our mind in the people, places, things, times, and events in our life. When we have purged the fear from ourselves, then even our children will not give us any reasons to be concerned.

We can learn from those unique individuals who have purged

the fear from their own lives. Those who are fearless have the freedom to explore the adventures of life without hesitation or concern. This freedom liberates one from a genetic life of routine into a transcendent, mystical life.

"As we are liberated from our own fear,
our presence automatically liberates others."

Nelson Mandela

Chapter 7

DARK NIGHT OF THE SOUL

In October 1985 I had just completed my last project, a training program with Robbins Research Institute in Snowmass, Colorado. Three months prior to this program I had given notice to my partners and told them that it was time for me to move on to a new adventure. The company was managed and developed into a very profitable institution within the eighteen months of me being involved, and the projections for success on every level were very optimistic. This financial opportunity, combined with the friendships that had been developed and the enormous success of a relatively new company, made it a difficult decision to leave. However, it was a decision that I had to make in order to move to my next level of evolution.

The day I left was a beautiful fall day in Southern California. It was sunny and cool. I had my car packed, a classic 1974 Mercedes 450 SL. I put the *St. Elmo's Fire* cassette tape in my stereo and in great joy drove out of Del Mar, California to the freeway on I-5 heading north. My destination was twenty-five driving hours away to my house overlooking the ocean in Washington State, a hundred and seventy miles south of the Canadian border.

The two-story house was situated on one-third acre perched on a two-hundred-foot cliff overlooking the shipping lanes of cargo ships traveling to and from Seattle and Tacoma. The last one hour of the trip was driving my car onto a large ferry that crossed five miles of ocean to the Kitsap Peninsula northwest of Seattle. It was on this same ferry crossing several years before that I watched the most beautiful sunset I had ever seen. It defied description and I was stunned at just seeing it. The final twenty-minute ride, a long highway that is bordered on both sides by one-hundred-foot evergreen trees, took me to my house located on Sunrise Beach Drive in Kingston, Washington. I had made this trip five or six times before and I always had the same ecstatic feeling of freedom as I drove into the driveway of this pristine house located on a cliff amongst tall evergreen trees.

Many afternoons and nights were spent sitting on the deck enjoying the feeling of drinking wine, beer, or Margaritas. I would often spend hours looking at the trees, the ocean, and gliding eagles on their way to the beach to hunt for fish. This was a time for long contemplation. Who was I going to be and what was I going to do when I grew up?

There is a part of the brain that can facilitate any request. It is called the reptilian brain, the oldest part of the brain. We refer to it in school as the lower cerebellum. It was the part of the brain that sent Einstein the information regarding his contemplations of gravity and light. This information was in response to his question as a twelve-year-old about the headlamp on his bicycle. My question about what I was going to become was answered in no less a dramatic way.

One afternoon, several days after arriving on this last trip, I joined two of my friends for lunch at a local restaurant forty-five minutes away. When they asked me what I wanted to drink, I passed, saying I wasn't feeling that great. We finished lunch fairly quickly and I had the feeling I was getting the flu. It came on me in moments and without any warning. My friends took me home and I went to bed that afternoon. As I lay in bed I became progressively more ill. It was a feeling I had never experienced before.

My exercise program for over ten years was long-distance running. I ran from three to twelve miles a day, at least five days each week, and often all seven days. I had not been sick for as long as I could remember. I never got a cold, a fever, or any symptoms that resembled being sick. It was for the most part a foreign experience, so lying in bed with these flulike symptoms was unusual and frightening.

My condition at night was terrifying. I would wake up in the middle of the night sweating and in fear. I became convinced that I was dying. After the long hours of sweating and fearful thoughts, I was so weak in the morning that it would take me two hours to get to the bathroom, which was located just across the hall. I would take long baths and pray that I might somehow recover from this downward spiral of vitality.

After twenty-three days of not eating, as I could not even fathom putting something into my mouth, a friend of mine suggested that I make an appointment to see a doctor. I had lost twenty-five pounds and looked very emaciated. I looked at him and said, "I am afraid I will believe what the doctor says." And I never made that appointment.

It was during these long and frightening nights that I began to review my life. I made a phone call to a friend in Hawaii and apologized for secretly spending time with his wife. During this long conversation we talked about God, our relationship to God, and that there was a more honorable way to live life. The beginning of my change came with this confession.

The next day I asked a friend of mine, who was staying at my house, what he thought I should do. I don't remember ever asking for his advice prior to this, but I was looking for answers anyplace I could find them. He simply suggested that I do what I had done that I enjoyed prior to getting ill. With that I grabbed a banana and a beer and forced them down my throat. To my surprise, they remained there. Within an hour I decided to walk down the road to the beach. I walked very deliberately and slowly. It was a most unusual experience. It was as if I had never done this walk before. Everything looked different and more vibrant. I was just happy to be alive with enough energy to walk. I came to a large rock on the beach and I sat on it. I made a covenant with God that day. If I were allowed to live, I would fully dedicate my life to understanding my relationship to God. With this deal in mind, I walked back to my house. From that day forward I began to regain my strength. It took over a year to fully recover.

When I decided to leave Southern California and begin a new adventure, I had no idea how radical a change that would become. But as I look back on it, I realize that anything short of a dramatic experience would not have given me the need to contemplate and change. Our God, housed in the lower cerebellum, has the wisdom to construct reality in such a way as to answer my request of what I would become when I grew up, and I continue to refine my relationship with God as I had promised over twenty years ago.

The dark night of the soul is an adventure that most people would not consciously create for themselves. It is highly adverse by its very nature, frightening in its experience, and ultimately freeing in its aftermath.

"Character cannot be developed
in ease and quiet."

Helen Keller

Chapter 8

MIRACLES AND MANIFESTATION

"One stormy night in the late sixties a friend was driving back to college. His van hit an oil slick and rolled over several times. The next thing he knew he was above the accident looking down at his body, and he knew that his body was so badly injured that it would be impossible for him to return to it. He was immediately moving into a film of light when he had one thought. The thought was, 'I have a choice.' This is the amazing part. In an instant he was back in his body but now the body didn't have a scratch on it, not even a bruise, and he was standing on the road watching his van burn. Another driver stopped and said to him, 'There is no hope for anyone to have survived this accident. What should we do?' My friend just said, 'I am the survivor.' What happened? Do you have an explanation?"

I absolutely do. This is an excellent example of the power of mind as matter. What happens in either a near-death experience or an out-of-body experience when you are in the infrared realm, is that you have the ability to look down into the Hertzian realm, which is our accustomed, three-dimensional reality.

Near-death experiences and profound out-of-body experiences radically change the makeup of the brain. In the infrared realm the mind is in a faster speed of creating reality.

Mind has the power of immediate reconstruction. His realization that he had a choice bumped him into a new timeline and on this line of reality he had miraculously survived the crash without injury.

There are two things that have the most profound effect on people that radically changes their brains. The first is a near-death experience. A person who has had this experience lives life quite differently from those who have not. There is no fear of death and at the same time an enormous appreciation of the simplicity of life itself. They exhibit a profound peace and there is always ample time to get everything done. The second thing is a UFO abduction. It has even been suggested that during this process you can download a whole new mind-set. That should certainly change a few things.

RSE is a School of Ancient Wisdom that promotes radical change, and our teacher will go to great lengths to get our attention. Many of the students in our school will eventually have the kinds of profound experiences I have just described.

"My father had a heart attack on October 31, 2003, where my brother and I had to give CPR until help came. We were told that his heart had stopped and we were not sure how long he was without air and that he might not make it. It has been almost two weeks since this happened. He has told us about a place he visited that was a two-story building, very cold and dark, old people were being evil, and they were chanting. He described it as voodoo-type people. A woman with two faces, one good and one evil, came to him. I would like to know what all this means and if you could help me."

There is a level of frequency just above our physical reality that is called infrared. With the stopping of his heart, he would be experiencing the symptoms of predeath or a near-death experience. However, instead of going to the light realm he stopped in the infrared realm. This realm is filled with earthbound entities who are still living as if they are alive on

Earth. These are the apparitions seen in old houses and are often called ghosts. It is a realm of addicted personalities that refuse to progress or do not know that they must continue their journey to the light in order to continue their evolution. What your father saw were those entities who are "stuck" in this realm of reality and do not have the knowledge necessary to move on.

This infrared level of reality is as "real" to the entities who inhabit that realm as this physical level of reality is to us. We can occupy a body on each level of reality and because that body is indigenous to that realm, it will seem as real there as our body does here. Whatever vibrates at the same frequency will be similar and equally physical in that realm of reality. You will not be able to pass through a wall in infrared if you are occupying an infrared body. The wall will be solid to your similarly vibrating body.

An out-of-body experience does not take place outside of the body. An out-of-body experience takes place within the body as you occupy one of your other six bodies. This is exactly what happens every night when you go to sleep. Your dreams are often fragmented images sent from your greater mind to heal your body through the firing of neurons in your brain that regenerate your cells in the areas of your body where healing is needed. While this process is taking place, your body is in a catatonic state. It is during this period of rejuvenation that you are free to travel and discover worlds that are associated with the other six realms of reality.

"Do all the entities in infrared see the light realm but just don't go there?"

No. They can only see the level of frequency that is slower than their own. That is why infrared entities can still stay associated with the Earth and their previous experience. Human beings without knowledge and training will only see the objects in this Hertzian frequency. However, with training you will begin to see dimensional entities from other levels of reality.

The beauty of knowledge is that it gives us options. There

is not one person who has this knowledge who will get stuck in infrared on their way to the light.

When we went to Cadaques, Spain in 2001, Ramtha was able to see that because of the religious influence there that many entities who had died did not have the knowledge of the planes of reality and were "stuck" in infrared. Many of those had died in Christ and were still waiting for his return. These entities are waiting in infrared. So Ramtha's message to the students who attended that Retreat was his teaching on evolution and the necessity for progressing beyond infrared to the light and to the "days of judgment." Those in infrared had the opportunity to hear his message and to act upon it if they desired.

When Ramtha was asked if he would return to Cadaques, Spain, he said that he would because it was a nodal place that would allow entities to get educated about the light, which would then afford them an option to move on in evolution.

Knowledge is so important. Without it, countless souls are still stuck in infrared waiting for someone to give them enough information to move on. That area of Spain, once the Languedoc area now in the country of France, has had its share of persecution by the Catholic Church. It takes a hierophant like Ramtha to release all of those souls that are imprisoned by their own ignorance. This is why knowledge is so important.

"What is the process of how our dreams come into our life after we focus on them in our C&E® sessions without doing anything? Why does it take people so long, even when they are longtime students, to manifest things like fabulous wealth, a house, etc., not to mention extraordinary phenomena?"

Existing in each person right now is a set of programs in the brain called neuronets. These are groups of thoughts tied together, and we call them attitudes. These attitudes initiate the programs housed in the brain, and these programs roll out the realities that we enjoy or from which we suffer. In order to create something really remarkable, we must transcend these programs in order to insert a new program.

The C&E® breath is used by students at RSE to anesthetize the existing programs so that something new can be introduced without an objection from the existing attitudes. Without the action of the breath, the existing programs will always object to an introduction of a new idea. Remember, no old regime that is in power will easily give up its control to a new regime no matter how brilliant the ideas of the new regime.

Once the existing programs are freeze-framed in the portion of the brain called the neocortex, the new idea can be focused upon without distraction, and consciousness, with this new idea, can easily move to the parts of the brain responsible for manifestation. The reason we don't chase dreams is because that would indicate that we do not have those realities, and that would be exactly what would be created: the chasing and not the experiencing.

When we create a new reality, we need to move consciousness (awareness) to the parts of the brain that exist in a time much different than linear time. We call these the quantum parts of the brain and they exist in the present moment, the timelessness needed to create a reality that has the effect of already existing. Therefore it manifests as a current reality and not as the chasing of a reality.

The reason fabulous wealth can be a difficult manifestation is that while one is creating this reality, simultaneously every other aspect of one's current reality is showing the signs of lack, and these override the newly created manifestation that is in the process of moving into a timeline. Remember, the internal picture of fabulous wealth must be more real than the environment and its "illusionary" reality. All realities are illusionary because they can be dreamed away. Fabulous wealth, in particular, requires holding onto that dream in spite of all that is being reflected back in one's environment. If that dream is steadfast, its reality is as certain as the laws of gravity.

Here is a great question that is typical of someone with a formal education.

"One of the reasons I am going to college is that I have the mind-set that before I can have wealth I must go to school to get a good job and a consistent paycheck. I have heard that to manifest something, you have to enter the state of mind that you already have it. If I already had wealth, I would not be going to school. So in order to manifest fabulous wealth, do I have to walk out on everything that reminds me that I don't already have it, like going to school?"

First of all, a consistent paycheck will never bring you fabulous wealth and, secondly, you do not have to walk out on anything, as those things will leave you once you have adopted this new state of mind.

If you hold the idea and concept that you are already fabulously wealthy, in spite of the environment and its reflections, your world and its content will change. The Observer effect in quantum physics says that whatsoever we see (observe) shall become the quality and the landscape of our lives. Our greatest temptation is to believe our current environment while it is still in the midst of changing into the new reality. Rarely do we have the persistence to hold onto the dream until it fully manifests. How long will it take? What I am going to tell you now is one of my greatest discoveries. It happens the moment you make up your mind that you are going to become this, no matter how long it takes and no matter what obstacles you have to encounter. The moment this commitment is made in your mind is the moment it manifests instantly. And why? Because your God knows that you have already accepted this new state of mind and will be it into eternity if necessary. Fabulous wealth or any other dream will take only as long as it takes for this state of mind to be fully adopted. As Ramtha says, "In a moment you can change," and as a friend of mine has said for many years, "Getting it is easy. It is not getting it that takes the time."

If we use an iceberg as an analogy of our reality, the part that we see is our hopes and dreams and the thoughts of our potential manifestations. The part that is under water, the greatest portion, is our true thoughts, and these attitudes are neurologically wired to the subconscious mind. It is this part of the brain that continues to observe these programmed thoughts into our life.

The Great Work teaches us how to reobserve the circumstances we want to change in our life and present these new potentials in an analogical state to our Observer. This focused concentration is an art and practiced skill that allows us the ability to make changes. Without knowledge you are going to assume that life is a random event generator and that some days work out better than other days.

"How can one heal the body instantly? What is the most powerful affirmation one can say to stay in the unlimited divine mind to have the power to heal instantly?"

The two questions work together perfectly, because in order to answer the second question you have to understand energy. In Ramtha's model, there are seven levels of mind in all of creation, from Point Zero, the highest level of consciousness and energy, all the way down to Hertzian, the lowest level of consciousness and energy. Point Zero in physics is called zero-point energy. It is the most powerful energy, and physicists are devoting an enormous amount of time working on how to harness it. The company or country that can get access to this energy and utilize it with an application is the company or country that will have dominion over everyone else. For more detailed information, please refer to Ramtha's book, *A Beginner's Guide to Creating Reality*.

Hertzian energy, the lowest frequency of the seven levels or environments, is the environment you and I enjoy each day. The energy of the Hertzian plane vibrates at a speed that is equal to the solidity of walls, rocks, tables, and the human body. Each level above the Hertzian energy, which can be called frequency, vibrates at a faster and faster rate. This frequency and its rate are what distinguish one level from another. Consciousness and energy simply means that what you think and the intent of those thoughts are what create the quality and the circumstances of your life.

Healing another person or yourself instantly requires that you be in a focused state of consciousness and energy that creates reality that has dominion over the physical body. The physical body is vibrating at the Hertzian level. The next two levels above Hertzian are infrared and visible light. Both of these levels of reality operate within a polarized environment. Visible light is the environment of photonic energy and is characterized by the polarity of positive and negative, the components of electricity.

All disease is the result of polarized thoughts that are judgments, opinions, or limited conclusions. These attitudes, coupled with the by-product of emotions, are what affect the health of the body. Therefore in order to heal a physical body you must move into a state of mind that is beyond polarized thought, which is the ultraviolet-blue realm. This frequency has dominion over the three frequencies below it. When you learn how to access this level of mind, you have the power to heal with a touch.

The story of the resurrection of a fish is an example of this technique. While in South Africa in 2001, I was saying good-bye to two of our teachers who were on their way to teach morning disciplines. Debbie, our Master of Music and teacher of frequency, yells to me, "We killed the fish!" I looked out on the patio and there in the pond was a fish that was looking straight up into the sun with that stare of death. There was not a drop of water in the pond, not even a wet spot where it was still evaporating. When we came back from our last class the night before, we turned off the lights on the patio and we must have turned off the power to the water pump at the same time.

Without thinking I placed a sacred symbol upon the fish. In the next instant I thought I saw its mouth move, but my brain convinced me it was just my imagination. Then I saw it move again. I was stunned and couldn't move. Then I heard Debbie say, "Go get it some water!" It was only then that I came out of my focus and could function enough to use a one-quart plastic container to begin filling the pond. By the time Debbie and Mike came back from the morning disciplines, the fish was once again swimming in its pond.

The symbol I used is associated with the ultraviolet-blue realm. I had been taught about the healing power of this level of reality and how to use it for restoration. You cannot use an affirmation to get this kind of result. An affirmation is used to overcome a predominant condition. We say we are radiant health when we are sick and need help. We say we are fabulously wealthy when we are in debt. These affirmations said in this way actually empower the condition we are trying to divorce ourselves from because we are acknowledging that these conditions exist and are the actual realities of our life.

Our school teaches how to create reality by becoming the very circumstance that you want to experience. We call this analogical mind, and this was the state of mind that I was in with the fish. However, there are underlying conditions that prevent most of us from creating extraordinary realities.

A large common denominator is unworthiness. In other words, we don't feel that we deserve to be that uncommon and powerful. Much of this attitude comes from conditioning, whether we were churchgoers or not. Many of us still have the thought that only God can do these things.

If you understand the historical perspective recorded in the Sumerian texts nearly ten thousand years ago, we now know that the Gods, the Elohim, as recorded in the Bible, intervened in our human evolution by manipulating the DNA of primitive man. This process of genetic manipulation began over 455,000 years ago, according to Ramtha. This intervention and our relationships as human beings to those Gods created attitudes of insecurity, unworthiness, and subservience that are still alive and well today in the DNA of human beings.

When humanity has these attitudes programmed into its genetic code, it is easy to see why we find it difficult to perform acts generally reserved for God or one of God's representatives, such as Yeshua ben Joseph, better known as Jesus the Christ. But Jesus did say, "These things that I do, you can do, and greater."

However, you will be hard-pressed to find a church that agrees that this statement should include you or me.

The Schools of Ancient Wisdom preceded training by first giving knowledge. With knowledge the student understands why change is necessary and, more importantly, what the outcome will be if there isn't change. To understand the attitudes of resistance to being great allows us to supersede this condition. Awareness always precedes control. With this understanding of why human beings limit the use of their power, it is possible to correct this long misunderstanding of why human beings experience a general sense of unworthiness.

Before I came to school and learned about my greater nature, I was building an empire of acquired assets because these things defined me. I defined myself by my accomplishments and by my acquisitions. I was operating under the "more is better" standard of living. I owned three homes, but because I only used the homes on occasion, I rented a fourth house on the beach as my principal residence. I had investments in Arabian show horses and that allowed me to travel to the horse shows so that I had something to do on a few weekends each year. I had the resources of time and money to pursue my own dreams, but my dreams included buying things to stave off my boredom. I eventually came to the understanding that this way of life was a dead end, literally. I asked myself, "Am I going to buy another home that I will not live in?" I suddenly realized that acquiring assets was not a life-sustaining activity, nor did it accurately define me as a human being. This began my quest for more meaning in my life.

"What is antimatter and its role in creating reality?"

This is an excellent question. Anytime that we take a two-dimensional concept such as an image, a picture, or a word that we want to manifest into our three-dimensional reality, we must take into consideration its positive and negative aspects. Everything in our perceived reality is composed of positive and negative charges. The very atoms that comprise all matter have positive charges in the nucleus and negative charges in the electron shells, so when we are creating reality we become aware that the image we are focusing on is the positive aspect of our intent, which corresponds to matter. What makes that two-dimensional image become a part of our three-dimensional reality and experience is its mirror image or what is termed its antimatter aspect. The Rosicrucian Order and other ancient schools before them used a mirror as a tool for manifestation. If you look into a mirror and raise your right hand, it will appear as if you are raising your left hand. That mirror is reflecting the antimatter aspect of what is looking into it.

The proper use of the brain takes a two-dimensional image and projects it holographically into the frontal lobe, the portion of the brain responsible for intention. A hologram is a three-dimensional image. If focused upon without distraction it creates the three-dimensional experience for the one who is observing. This process of transmutation from a two-dimensional image into a three-dimensional image is critical for creating an experience. If the image remains two-dimensional, then rather than creating fabulous wealth you would get a postcard (two dimensions) from a friend who took a picture of you standing in front of the Hotel Bel Air that is frequented by the very rich and famous. A postcard is a different experience than registering as a guest at the hotel.

We can manifest reality by pretending. If we continue to pretend long enough, we will have fired the neurons in a specific portion of the brain that the Observer will facilitate by the same law that says, "What ye sow, ye shall reap." So pretending will lead to manifestation if done long enough to create the neuronet in the brain. Pretending is one of the processes that great actors use to create a character. To stay "in character" is the process that hardwires a neuronet into an attitude. An attitude, unless it is changed, becomes a permanent part of one's personality. As we have been taught, the personality is a group of automatic programs that can be turned on by a thought.

There are many studies that have shown that pretending is as powerful in building a skill as the actual practice. Both activities utilize the brain in the same manner. Science has shown that the brain does not know the difference between what is actually being practiced and what is being imagined as practice. There are published reports with kids shooting free throws with a basketball and most recently a study involving the learning of how to play a piano. Regarding the basketball study, they divided the kids into three groups. All the kids shot a certain amount of free throws to establish a baseline of performance. I do not remember the exact criteria, but it was something like group number one had to shoot twenty-five free throws twice a day for two weeks, group number two was to imagine shooting twenty-five free throws twice a day for two weeks, and group number three did nothing. At the end of two weeks, group number three had not improved but groups number one and number two had improved equally as well. This concentrated focus, combined with a visualization technique, is the key to creating new realities using consciousness. The brain works in a very specific way, and both practice and the imagination of practice work equally well.

Many great athletes are known for their work with visualization. Until recently Phil Mickelson was known as the best golfer never to win a major tournament. He has attributed some of his recent success to his work with visualization. To win the Masters Tournament, arguably the greatest golf tournament each year, he had to sink an eighteen-foot putt. It is fair to say that he visualized his ball going into that hole several times before he actually hit the putt. So in essence he had three or four tries to sink his putt.

In our school we use visualization only after having prepared the brain properly to accept this new idea. All new ideas are going to elicit some resistance from the brain. As we have seen with the children of the Bronx, new ideas are only accepted if the impact of that idea can be easily predicted. If the impact cannot be predicted, then we must prepare the brain in a specific way to accept this idea. Visualization without proper preparation of the brain is a time-consuming and ineffective activity. It will work, but you should be prepared to be very patient. Preparing the brain properly bypasses this resistance to change and we often have immediate results. This is why one would want to go to a school that teaches this knowledge.

"How does what you have just described differ from affirmations?"

Affirmations are used without the knowledge of how to optimize their power. In most cases people get the opposite of what they begin to affirm. The very act of creating an affirmation states emphatically that you do not have what it is that you are affirming. According to the Observer effect in quantum mechanics, you will continue to do without it. If someone uses an affirmation to overcome a circumstance such as financial lack or poor health, the chances of change are very small. Remember the statement, "As within, so without." You must become what it is that you want to experience. Affirmations are often used like prayer. The moment you are affirming something or praying for something that is separate from you, it must remain separate from you because you have created it that way in its application. Affirmations and prayers are done because you need something that you do not have. This is so important. If you understand the difference between asking for something that you do not have and becoming something that you want, you will have the key to the kingdom of heaven. At this point the obvious question would be: How do you become something that you want? And the answer is: Go to a school that teaches this knowledge.

When you realize that everyone in our culture has attention deficit disorder, which is called ADD, then you begin to realize why being able to hold a single focus without distraction is called a mastery. According to some recent studies, most people are distracted six to ten times each minute. So in the beginning, the disciplines are being practiced with new desires that are competing against attitudes that have been established for twenty, thirty, or more years of acceptance. The distraction comes from the existing neuronets that might be replaced with these new ideas and potential realities. This battle will go on between the existing regime and the new regime that is calling for a paradigm shift. If you persist in these disciplines with any new idea, they will eventually win this battle. A new neurological neuronet will be formed, which is the new regime in power, and the distractions will fade away. This is precisely how we make changes in our life.

"I believe that invisibility is possible, but do you know the secrets of how to alter the laws of physics?"

You don't alter the laws of physics; you comply with them. What you are referring to is classical physics, a four-hundred-year paradigm, and of course none of those classical laws can explain some of the esoteric phenomena. However, the new science of quantum mechanics and its Observer effect allow for all thoughts to be experienced as reality, which includes invisibility. The secret is not in the law that allows exotic phenomena but in the knowledge that it is possible and the discipline that becomes the infrastructure for its experience.

"Is there one thing I can do to get unstuck from the inertia that ensnares me? I was downsized three years ago. I lost my home and medical. I have yet to find any work because I am either over- or underqualified for the positions. I am 58 years old and I no longer recognize the person staring back at me in the mirror. I go to a metaphysical church, but I am getting more and more discouraged because of the long list of unanswered prayers."

When you understand that what you think matters — in fact, what you think *is* matter — then you will understand why your prayers are not getting answered. The first thing you are caught up in is the daily reminder of your own lack. You are observing your environment — it is showing you the lack — and that continues to reinforce its reality. You will need to break this obvious cycle of seeing yourself this way. You cannot depend on your eyes to do this for you, as they will only betray your new intent.

What we learn in school is how to become what we want to experience. This now becomes our daily prayer. Every time we think about this new experience we give thanks to the intelligence within us that is opening the doors to this opportunity. We have been taught to do this every day until it manifests in our life. If our commitment is to do this until it manifests, we will activate the part of our brain that has the power and the authority to observe this thought into physical reality. We learn how to do this in our school, and the results seem unbelievable because it is so simple. If you end up coming to school, you will learn the exact science of this process. Science is important because it erases the doubt that always undermines the new dream.

"Can you explain what is involved in daily focus?"

Daily focus is about having created your day and holding that intent as it unfolds throughout the day. We have included disciplines at our school that reinforces this idea of holding an intent throughout the entire day. When we do our Neighborhood Walk^{SM} at an event, we will do this walk five or six times each day. If you are remembering something that you want to create that often, then you are lessening the amount of time each day in which you have forgotten what you are creating. All of the disciplines in the school are to sharpen the student's ability to hold a thought for a period of time without distraction. If you can learn to do this, you will have mastered the fundamental skill for manifesting any experience into your life.

"Can you talk about karma and using the different parts of the brain to create different realities? This is about finding a new job. Maybe you are in a job because karmically this is where you are supposed to be. Will wanting to set an intent to find a new job in which you will be happier be ineffective? In other words, does karma take precedence over setting an intent that you want to manifest?"

Nothing takes precedence over setting an intent and

manifesting that reality through persistent observation. There is no karma that takes precedence over a new dream. Karma simply means that you have unfinished business. That is your karma. It is this mind-set that continuously objects to new thoughts and new dreams because they threaten the predictable and existing reality. That is where karma has an effect on getting a new job. It shows up by literally talking you out of certain opportunities. This mind-set will endeavor to remind you of all the security being offered in the old job and the possible pitfalls that are lurking in the shadows of the new, unpredictable opportunity. This is precisely what happened to the children of the Bronx and the internal dialogue that went on in each of their heads.

"I am a businessman and my bother has told me that some of the individuals in your community have created fabulous opportunities for wealth, including paying off their homes very quickly. Can you tell me how these feats have been accomplished? I don't understand how you become wealthy without working thousands of hours of overtime."

First of all, you have given me the reason why you could not become wealthy. You have wealth dependent upon a work load that is conventional reasoning. You could not work enough hours of overtime to become wealthy. In addition, overtime is not a concept that is incorporated in the mind of one who is wealthy.

These opportunities of fabulous wealth have been accomplished in a myriad of ways but the methodology is the same for everyone. When I decided to become sovereign, I made some sacrifices that eliminated living a lifestyle that was left over from my past. However, the moment I made this new lifestyle change, circumstances began to unfold to manifest my intent to become sovereign. I had received some money from an inheritance but it had been put into a trust that did not allow me full access to it for twenty years. I made a card, focused on it, and did not waiver in my intent even when I was told that it was inaccessible. To make a long story short, I got all of the money in increments over seven years, including my home being paid in full.

What is beautiful about opportunities is that they are made from the mind of the one who is holding the dream. What seems at once impossible becomes probable through the organization of the quantum field to create that reality. So the methodology is the same, which is an Observer, you or me, holding a dream in absolute resolution until it manifests. There are numerous stories of similar manifestations and they always come in unexpected ways. As long as you do not try to figure out how this manifestation will unfold, you will be handing it over to the part of the brain that has the proper tools to accomplish the job. If you do not waiver, even though your environment is showing you a different reality, you will be triumphant every time. I did not let a complicated legal agreement have power over my own conviction, and that became obvious shortly after the trust was filed. Imagine the level of acceptance that is accrued with a few victories. There is nothing that can stand in the way of a willful person who has the tenacity to hold onto a dream.

If you were walking in a field and you found several pieces of gold, what would you do? Most people would quickly calculate the price of gold and multiply it by the number of coins to get a total. That would be the thinking of a person who works mass to mass to create their reality. An enlightened being would see if the property were for sale and buy it, knowing that it was frequency specific to gold and would continue attracting that reality. The difference in these two approaches is the difference between a one-time opportunity and continuous wealth.

Willful intent is absolute. There is no room for anything but the manifestation of the idea. Effort and trying will get you exactly those attitudes. Effort implies that what you are attempting to create is beyond acceptance and will always require more. Therefore you will never be successful with something that requires more. When you try, you will always get the effects of trying but never the accomplishment. Trying implies that you are in an uphill battle. You will not become the dream while trying. All that is available to you is the experience of trying. Every person can remember circumstances in their life in which they tried to get something to happen. One is absolute while the other never accomplishes the outcome.

"Who can we tell about our dreams and who should we not tell? Should we keep secret what it is we are focusing on until it manifests?"

I would keep it secret from anyone you suspect might doubt or be jealous of your new idea. However, "two or more gathered together in my name, thy will be done" is an effective and synergistic method for accelerating a manifestation. Sharing a concept with those who are not aligned with your success can be considered an interference wave that undermines your dream, while the latter can be seen as frequency coherent and a way to amplify the probability of your new dream.

"Since it is true that to change an exterior reality we must first change an interior reality, why must we go through the process of protesting against the abuse of the environment, cell phone towers, big box corporations, or NASCAR? Why not just focus on what you want? Why does it require a physical interaction?"

Manifestations occur according to expectations. Students in the school combine focus with action to create outcomes. We are not yet at the level of manifesting some of these realities without follow-up. Creating a reality will often open the doors of opportunity but you must still walk through the doors to get the prize or to be shown the next step. When a group of common people fight against large corporations, it is a battle of wills and we must fight on the same field as our opponents. We are dealing with the world on the terms of the world. This fight often requires our participation and physical interaction.

"Why can't we manifest an albatross in the sky that is

away from the shore even though we are the creators of our realities?"

It is very simple. You can't, because you don't think you can. The fact that you can say that you are a creator does not change your belief on its own. If you are the same person every morning asking for a new reality, you will not get the new reality. You can only manifest what is frequency specific to your mind. You must know that you are the creator of your reality. You will know this is true when your life is in accord with your new creations. We cannot change the taste of wine by putting new wine in an old wineskin. It will always taste like the old wineskin. We must put the new wine in the new wineskin. We must create our realities from our new mind.

"Do you have any tips on creating things in your life? All of the things I have manifested in my life are not really major goals. They have been small things that were not so important to me, but I can manifest those very quickly. My major goals that I spend lots of time thinking about never manifest. Give me some tips to stop sabotaging myself."

The answer is in your statement. Here is the tip: Do exactly with your major goals as you do with those manifestations that are not as important. When you put importance on a goal, you automatically assume it is going to be a battle because it's so important. And of course it ends up being almost impossible to create.

It is common thoughts that are easily and rapidly manifested into reality. You must treat your important goals in the same manner that you create those small things that you manifest very quickly. When we work on manifestations, we work on them over and over until we are almost bored with the concept. Boredom is a sign that the concept is becoming a common thought, and it is common thoughts that manifest rapidly.

"Why would Ramtha have students focus on several

things at a time when most of the literature says to focus on one thing until it manifests and then move on to something else?"

Even when we are creating more than one thing at a time, each item gets our undivided attention as if it were the only thing we were focusing on.

"I started out with an idea to win lots of contests, and it worked. I would like to win bigger things like cars. How can I make it happen? If luck is not the ingredient, how do people win the lottery?"

There are no coincidences. Everything is intentional. "God does not play dice," Einstein said. He was right, but not for the reference in which he was using that statement. Every person who has won the lottery has prepared themselves for its manifestation. You do not need to know that consciousness and energy creates the nature of reality to create reality. We are always creating the circumstances of our lives with our thoughts, neurological programs, and attitudes. If you pursue something long enough, it will find its way into your life.

If you can win small contests, then you can win big contests with the same attitude you used with the small contests. If you can develop a greater level of acceptance, you can create a greater level of reality. Sometimes it is difficult to win big contests, manifest large items, or create the ideal partner because you have a program about not being worthy of that level of success. You must become the person who would have no problem with any of these manifestations. So how would you have to change in order to be the person who would live a life you have asked about? If you can act like that person and stay in character long enough, you will activate the neuronet or attitude that is required to accept and create those manifestations. I would inundate my brain with pictures, articles, and books that would inspire me to think in those new ways. The janitor who wins the multimillion-dollar lottery, though it will look like luck or coincidence, is someone who dreamed for many hours about the possibility of winning. They dreamed to the point that it became acceptable. You must do the same thing with what it is you want to create.

"Can you fix appliances with the techniques of the school?"

I have on several occasions. I was asked to fix a washing machine that was making terrible gear-crunching noises. It took about thirty seconds using a sacred symbol and I was done. My two friends said, "Is that it?" I said, "That's it. I'm expensive." It has continued to work perfectly up to this moment, which has been over five months.

"If I can get the picture of what I want to create with my eyes closed, do I add an emotion to that picture or do I simply observe it as if detached?"

If we add an emotion, it can only come from a past experience and we would be concluding what this new reality would feel like. We can never know what the experience is going to be if we are making known the unknown. So if we can observe the picture as if detached, then it can manifest and unfold in unexpected ways with unexpected emotions. The Observer is the only one qualified to manifest a desire as an evolutionary experience. Any added emotion would require the neocortex to get involved, and that is the part of the brain that cannot manifest an evolutionary experience. It can only reproduce what has already been experienced.

"Is it true that students have grown back new teeth? How did they do it? Did they take any supplements?"

I know the lady in our school who grew back two of her teeth after twenty years of having no teeth. She left school soon after her medical miracle about five years ago and moved back to Australia. Whenever I got questions about this I had to say that I did not know how to get in touch with her so that she could tell her story. However, I just happened to see her at a gas station last week and wanted to look at the two teeth to make sure they were still there. She has just moved back, so I can get her to tell her story in more detail. I do not know what disciplines she used specifically, but in our school you have many to choose from to create a reality. When she was a current student, we did a lot of healing work during those years, so I am going to surmise that the healing work was a large part of the disciplines that she did. She is the only student I know who has grown back her third set of teeth.

It takes a lot of knowledge to get from a cause-and-effect world that is perceived by the senses to a quantum world of all possibilities that is beyond the senses, but it is this very shift that allows for the third set of teeth to be regrown and other miracles of a similar magnitude. Our world is a construction of the people, places, things, times, and events that are produced from our mind. If you change your mind, you change the principal elements of your environment. Every discipline in our school is designed to create new experiences that expand our mind and change our world.

"Can you describe the trance state and why it is effective in manifesting new realities?"

It is effective because it does not judge the new concept as unrealistic, positive, negative, or threatening. In its neutrality it allows for the unfolding of this new idea without having to edit it. The trance state is the result of moving your awareness or attention out of the neocortex. We are now neurologically disconnected from the neocortex that constantly judges, concludes, and objects to new ideas. The most important function of the neocortex is to help us make wise decisions that sustain the life of the organism. In doing this, it is constantly on the lookout for potential dangers. In our school we use different techniques to bypass this part of the brain so that we can facilitate a different level of consciousness and energy that easily includes the new manifestation. We know we are in a trance state when the idea that we are contemplating becomes more real than the environment in which that contemplation takes place. This is being in the present moment with your new idea. This is the secret to manifesting anything you want. It is the distractions of the environment, the body, and time that undermine these dreams of potential. Being in the present moment is a skill that can be taught and developed.

"Could a big challenge of harnessing our manifesting power be that we are so interconnected with our desires that they often include other people and their cooperation?"

No, but you might be surprised as to why. It is difficult to include those other people in your new reality because they are intimately connected to your old reality, and that becomes a neurological conflict of interest. Everyone in your life is frequency-specific to you and comes directly out of your mind. If you change yourself, then the people who are frequency-specific to your change will remain in your life and those that are not will leave. We never have to worry about including anyone or being concerned that we must include them. It is a reality that will be exclusive to your personal creations.

However, it is important to realize that we often use people as our excuse not to change and in that way those people that you are referring to may represent a challenge to you creating an elegant and efficient manifestation. If, however, you can realize that everything in your life is a projection from your own contemplations, your attitudes, and your thoughts, which together formulate your mind, then that understanding can often make it easier to change without the concern that those changes will have a detrimental effect on those around you. We do not use this understanding as a license to do unto others what we would not do to ourselves. "What goes around comes around" is a truth!

To further explain the quantum field and its glorious ability, if you ask your question with "could" or "is it possible," then that presupposes your own assumptions and the quantum field will respond accordingly. The quantum field does not give everyone the same answer; it responds according to one's own assumptions and expectations. That unique quality is how the quantum field empowers every human being by responding to their thoughts and attitudes. This field of all potentials is what the Christians call the kingdom of heaven and what the ancient philosophers called the mind of God. And in a more animated and contemporary reference it is the genie in the bottle that grants the wishes.

"It takes practice and skill to live without regret."

A Good Woman

Chapter 9

MASTERS

**"*The Life and Teachings of the Masters of the Far East*
were a romantic idea for me because I couldn't duplicate
what they were doing. I can't be that different. I mean, we
are all human beings. Is it that they have knowledge that
I don't have?"**

That is part of it. Once you have the desire to change, you
only need knowledge and training. The masters of the Far East
have great knowledge, but what they possess that separates them
from the mass of humanity is the desire to become something
they are not.

The Bible may have once said, long before the millenia of
translations, that Jesus told his followers in a literal sense, "These
things that I do, you can do, and greater." If you were to tell
your minister or priest that you were going to outdo Jesus, you
would be perceived as a fanatic and someone to watch from a
cautious distance. How inspired Jesus would have been to watch
his disciples doing great miracles. It would have meant that they
had heard what he had been saying, "It is the Father within me
that does these things, and that same Father is within you." No
master is ever intimidated by the success of his or her student.
It is a manifestation of their intent.

A listener told me that her husband had an alien encounter
about four months ago. In his words, he was taken from his bed

and returned later with wounds on his body. Since that time she has been getting calls from people from different parts of the world with similar experiences. She asked me what I thought. She told me she had no idea what to tell these people who were calling and asking how to prevent it from happening again, as it was bringing up so many fears.

I am always surprised to hear that a civilization with a mind that has the power to abduct humans, remove them from their premises, and return them without anyone knowing would bother to do so with human beings. I have heard and read about experiments that go on in alien crafts to extract DNA from humans because it has an emotional fabric that is missing from some alien cultures. So how do we prevent it from happening again? We always draw to us what we constantly focus on, whether that is riches, lack, or fear of aliens. To confront any fear is to disarm its power. Whether it is the government sending out this energy, or aliens completing some experiments, or an imagination that creates reality, it is stopped when you say, "Enough!" and mean it. When you have not made a decision, then there is room for manipulation. But nothing has the power to interfere with your decisions. Either consciousness and energy creates the nature of reality in all cases or it is not a law. As science is proving, it is the quintessential law of how reality is formulated.

A friend of mine was outside in his yard and without notice realized he was in an abduction scenario complete with alien craft and examination rooms. He explained that it was as real as daily living. When a "doctor" tried to examine him, he walked right over to "her" and looked into her eyes. She disappeared right in front of him. The next thing he knew, he was back in his bed with two hours missing. What he told me was that he wanted to confront this being and let her know whose mind was in charge, and with that the being vaporized. Most intelligent species honor commands from another God. Being fearless with the heart of a warrior delivers that intent without need for further discussion or negotiation. It is absolute! Ramtha has given us the secret to intimidate a bully or hostile situation. He says just look at them and get present. That is a disarming moment, and the superstitious mind of the one being looked at will become frightened and you will be free to go on your way.

"Ramtha has mentioned that other ascended masters have gone on to other realms rather than stay around and assist humans. Why did the other masters not stay around?"

They had a greater interest in themselves and their own journey rather than assisting those who still need help. Masters have no conscience that would persuade them to make a choice against their own personal desires, so very few stay and help. Ramtha is an exception. He made a promise 35,000 years ago and he is keeping that promise. Now for those few who did stay around, their message was destroyed or their lives discredited by those who had an investment in a different philosophy. Most people do not want help. Most people are happy with their own limited humanity. When you are without knowledge and you are genetically encoded by the soul to have certain propensities, you have a tendency to accept, tolerate, or rationalize those attitudes by saying that is who you are. This human condition of accepting your limitations is a great and secret disease.

"JZ has always been the first to acknowledge that she is a student of Ramtha, and the first one at that. Will she transcend?"

If you mean will she ascend, she has recently said that she has no interest in ascension while there is so much to experience just within this Hertzian plane. Remember, all the planets known and those to be discovered are all in the Hertzian plane, so there is a lot of living to be done before we get to that question.

"I have a question about Zen and our method. What I have been unable to understand is where or what Zen is referring to when they speak of entering the epicenter

of the present moment. Is that the same as Point Zero? If it is and if they just allow creation to unfold (that's my understanding of Zen), then which consciousness is creating the unfolding that they observe? Are both the Zen method and the Ramtha school compatible? Can you do both? How does a great Zen avatar compare to a master in Ramtha's teachings?"

The epicenter of the present moment is what we call the analogical experience. It is the moment that your concentrated thoughts or focus are without distraction. Point Zero is the ancient term for the Observer. The only thing the Observer ever observes is the neuronet that is being active at the time of observation. The consciousness that is creating the unfolding is housed in the neuronet that is being activated. This is what is meant by "What ye sow, ye shall reap." What you are thinking will be observed into your life.

The two methods are not compatible, with the following exception. If you use the Zen methods to reach that moment of being present, then you would want to shift your focus from the passive, letting it unfold to a more active process in which you can create something specific. The RSE methods are unique and specific for using the brain properly to create intentional realities. Without a specific intention, you would tend to continue creating the same reality from the same neuronet.

We calculate the greatness of any student by their ability to consciously manipulate reality on demand, so a great Zen avatar should be able to accomplish the disciplines of our school on a consistent basis. We test that ability at every event. We know who is accomplishing the disciplines and who is still practicing them.

Unfortunately, Buddhism has built into its philosophy an eternal reincarnation scenario. We know this because the Dalai Lama continues to reincarnate. Our philosophy has built into it the concepts of immortality, ascension, and conquering one's limitations. That is the philosophy of a true warrior.

"I am new to the teachings. How do you define a master? Are all masters immortal?"

My definition of a master is one who can consciously create reality on a consistent basis. It is a person who creates their day and observes it into reality. A master is never victimized by the circumstances of life but rather always responsible for that reality. Masters know that they are immortal already. These unique entities are always in control and will observe their intent into its manifested form, whatever that might be. However, living in a human body for eternity is not the desire of every master. In fact, it is the desire of very few masters. The human body is large, slow, and cumbersome. It is not a very efficient or attractive vehicle for going places or getting things done.

"Must everyone overcome and conquer death as Ramtha did?"

Of course not, but wouldn't it be nice if you had that option among a few others? Conquering the fear of death is a prerequisite to conquering death itself. The greatest inhibitor to joy within the human species is the fear of death. It undermines all of our hopes and dreams. Until the fear of death is owned, there will always be a reticence to live life to its fullest. The pinnacle achievement of a human being is the conquering of death. It is not a requirement. It is, however, a genuine option.

"Ramtha says that it takes a magnificent human being to become a master. Can you become a master in one life or must we go through many, many more?"

First of all, we have already gone through many, many lives. So we have handled the criteria of many, many more already. Ramtha became his magnificent self in one life. He did so by living it to its fullest. He has told us that becoming a master in these times is more difficult than in his own days because there are so many more forms of distraction now. However, it can be done in one concentrated, glorious life. As our teacher has said, "If it can be dreamed, it already is." And some of the students in our school are beginning to prove that.

"I just read a book that postulates that Jesus was stoned for stealing a sacred text. Did that happen?"

I have not heard that story. Without reading the book myself, I do not have the context in which the statement was made. Was there documentation to support the theory? Was it a parallel reality? We know from quantum physics that if the question can be asked, it already exists as a potential in the mind of God. Was anyone there to observe that slice of reality? This specific concept is not a mainstream, historical rendition that has appeared in any other texts. You will need to do the additional research for yourself.

"Is it the white powder of gold that is real magic? Is it Viktor Schauberger's theories on free energy or is the real magic belief?"

It is belief that is the real magic. Belief is what the Observer in quantum physics collapses into manifested reality. I am not talking about belief that is unfounded and conjecturous. I am defining belief as something in which someone is certain. If you look at the placebo effect in medicine, you will know that belief gives permission to the body to do what the pill only occasionally does.

The genius who created the white powder of gold did so out of his own belief, and of course the powder is going to produce extraordinary results because it became frequency- specific with his own expectations. The powder took on the mind of its creator. Viktor Schauberger's theories on free energy work because of his own research that supported his original belief. Both of these examples follow the laws of quantum physics perfectly. Whatsoever you believe, so shall you experience.

Quintessential alchemists who pursued their craft did so until they transmuted themselves into transcendent human beings. To turn base metals into gold was a stepping stone and only a secondary outcome. It was believed that one could fire base metals in a crucible with acids and salts until the liquid produced an extraordinary elixir that contained the mind of the alchemist's unwavering pursuit. That belief in transcendence was the catalyst for the alchemist to pursue his goal and to expand his mind. Nothing outside of itself will be as powerful as the mind that creates it, and belief is the secret key to activating the Observer to produce that reality.

"Can you reconcile the Earth being destroyed by ignorant people?"

Ramtha has said that "Whatever you feel strongly about, you have yet to own." This statement alone gives you an incredible insight into the mind of an expanded being.

Being angry will only reinforce the concept that things are out of your control and that one person does not have the power to effect change. If we engage what we love with passion, then the mind and the energy to make a difference will become apparent. If you knew that you were eternal, that your job was to own the emotions generally expressed in situations that still bother you, and that you existed to create new experiences, you could see the wisdom in being an Observer rather than engaging in emotional reaction. This state of beingness is more powerful and proactive than all the emotions that could be generated to accompany a cause.

"A rock pile ceases to be a rock
when somebody contemplates it
with the idea of a cathedral in mind."

Antoine de Saint-Exupéry
French Novelist

Chapter 10

RELIGIOUS LEADERS

"How do I begin my enlightenment?"

The greatest beginning to the path of enlightenment is to ask the question about enlightenment, so you are already on the journey to that understanding.

Ramtha is 35,000 years old and he came long before Christ, Mohammed, and all the other legendary beings. His teachings include the foundations of the Earth, the cosmos, and the journey of humanity from the beginning of time. He has seen a lot of history. Ancient wisdom predates all religions and all "isms," whether it is Islamism, Catholicism, Judaism, or any other ism. All of these organized religious movements came after Ramtha's life and all are interpretations of God's word, even though some claim to be the messenger or prophet of God. Ramtha has had the unprecedented view of watching each of these religions and their effect on humanity. None of these organized belief systems have been an enlightening factor to humanity and all have been warlords to protect their beliefs. As Ramtha has said, "No army has been more vicious than the Catholic Church."

When Ramtha talks about the current religions, he gives few compliments to any of them. None of the three major religions hold women as equals. This in itself shows their vast ignorance. The Jews have a separate section for the women when they come to temple, and with some of the Jewish sect a men does not sleep in the same bed as their wife when she is having her season of blood. The Muslims and even the Hindus will ostracize or even kill women that are perceived as unfaithful. Some Christian men still see their wives as the servants of themselves and often quote scripture to validate this.

Either we are Gods, endowed with a divine intelligence and a legacy that transcends gender, or we are not. With Ramtha being a quintessential master and knowing that divinity is within all human beings, you can understand why he is not impressed with any of the current religions. He said in an audience with his advanced students, and it is worthy to say again, that "Even the Buddhists do not allow their women to be the Dalai Lama."

I love the Dalai Lama. He is a simple man. I had the pleasure of seeing him at a conference in South Africa. But you have to ask yourself why, if he is the incarnating Buddha, he continues to incarnate with bad eyesight.

None of the established religions teach that God is within. If they did, they would be risking their congregations and none seem to be willing to do that for the sake of truth. The greatest document I have read on the history of humanity is in two volumes: *A Master's Reflection on the History of Humanity*, by Ramtha.

"Today I watched in sadness as people surrounded Arafat's coffin. I observed that there were no women in the crowd. I don't believe that it was because they didn't want to be there but because of suppression. I pointed this out to my nine-year-old daughter. However, the media did not consider it newsworthy to mention."

That was a very astute observation. I didn't get a chance to watch much of the procession. I was busy and occupied with RSE events in South Africa at that time. I am sorry that the passing of a significant and contemporary leader in this world is dominated by the respect of men without the support or acknowledgement of the importance of women. He was a Palestinian leader of great conviction, but it is my opinion that there is no such thing as a great leader without the mutual respect and admiration of the men and women that they serve. I believe that Mohammad had two great advisers: his wife and his military General. Maybe there is something missing in the contemporary version.

God is neither gender but represents both equally. When we see religious institutions that cater more to the needs of men and hold them in higher positions in the organization, we have control and ignorance. There will never be peace on Earth as long as this gender separation exists because ignorance is still greater than knowledge. How could there be a hierarchy with God? As Ramtha has told us, there is not gender separation in civilizations of greater mind. We are moving to a future in which equality is the accepted norm and those who cannot make this obvious shift will be left behind or simply pass away.

"I was raised Lutheran. Martin Luther broke from the church because he said that one did not need an intermediary to access the kingdom of heaven. So why does one have to go to the Ramtha School, especially when Ramtha had no other teacher except nature?"

The answer is simple. You are academically trained by teachers who know more than you in subjects in which they have earned the right of expertise. Regarding your training in the nature of reality, you also want to be trained by someone who knows more than you and has earned that right. The school is an environment that enhances one's knowledge and experience in the nature of reality. Martin Luther realized that the church inhibited one's access to God, and the intentional and consistent access to God is the purpose of RSE.

We can only experience what we have mapped in our brains through knowledge, genetics, and our own contemplations of inquiry. Einstein's constant contemplations led to the visions that set the stage for his theories of relativity. Constant pursuit and the genetics of a superior race are how Ramtha discovered the

Unknown God. We can see by history that only a few individuals make the kind of breakthroughs that lead to revolutionary understandings. Most human beings left to their own initiative will do little to evolve themselves spiritually. Most of us are distracted by making a living and being entertained by sports and spectacular breaking-news stories that are offered twenty-four hours every day. This is the same strategy employed by the Romans. While everyone was entertained by the activities in the coliseum, the Roman senate made new policies to their own advantage. The citizens did not care as long as they had a seat for their weekly entertainment.

To know something takes knowledge from a teacher or a preserved document of truth that is combined with an environment that can offer exercises or disciplines for the direct experience of that knowledge. Neither Martin Luther nor the church could answer the four great questions: Who am I? Where did I come from? What is my destiny? How do I accomplish that destiny? These questions require a teacher who has earned the right to answer them through direct experience. Even with a great teacher such as Yeshua ben Joseph, we are left with a document that is vastly different from his original teachings. So the greatest danger of not having a teacher or a document of truth is that one is left with superstition, interpretation, and dogma. We continue to see how easily organized religion manipulates the people who are without truth. That manipulation has been the greatest sin perpetuated on the human race. One of my favorite Ramtha quotes is, "I have the fortitude and the power to chnage the moon into gold, but that would pale if I could change people into Gods, and that is my mission." That puts into perspective the difficulty of this campaign.

"What have you come to understand about the Mormons? I am very curious because my girlfriend is an ex-Mormon."

The Mormons have a unique history that includes UFOs as part of that history. They are fully dedicated to their religious understandings with strong community and family values. They have been taught to be self-sufficient and to store food and water in times of instability. They have meticulously kept the genealogical records of their history. Their symbol is the beehive and they have that same kind of community work ethic.

They are, however, a male-dominated organization in which the women are supposed to be the support system rather than the leadership of the system itself. I have never experienced a male-dominated religion that was inspiring and joyful. The hierarchy is kept in place by rules and regulations, and this undermines any hope for real inspiration. When you have men who believe that they are the superior intellect, then you have a strong prejudice that can lead to practices like polygamy, which was allowed in the Mormon faith. Brigham Young, a hero in that organization, loved young women, and the joke was that he asked they "bring 'em young." When a leader needs that much attention, it is a sign that the knowledge and the experience of being in that organization are not satisfying. I would imagine that this dissatisfaction is alive and well in most religious organizations that depend on dogma rather than the direct experience of personal truth.

"I was recently invited to join the Freemasons. I don't know too much about them. Would you consider this a good group to get involved with?"

I would suggest that you go to a meeting. The fruit of the knowledge should be evident. If you find the information you learn and the quality of those who have experienced that information to be inspiring and hopeful, then you might want to continue. The Freemasons, at least historically, had access to great knowledge. I do not know if they have retained that knowledge or if they have simply replaced it with meaningless ritual. You should know after one or two meetings. We know from history that the Masons were a secret society and retained the sacred knowledge in their stone cathedrals. Those cathedrals still remain a source of knowledge for those who have the eyes to see.

It is worth repeating that when the sun pierces its light through the stained-glass windows, they cast a shadow on the cathedral floor. This is exactly how our brain processes information to manifest its reality from the quantum field. The sun represents the Observer. The stained-glass windows represent our different neuronets, and the shadow on the floor represents the unfolding of those potentials into our life. When the cathedral rotates to another stained-glass window in front of the sun, it casts a different shadow onto the cathedral floor and that represents a different reality. The shadow on the cathedral floor is the quality of life that depends on the content of the stained-glass window. The Masons knew that these truths would be very difficult to change if they were incorporated into huge stone cathedrals. They were familiar with the habit of rewriting documents and issuing them as new editions of older books newly translated to reflect the needs of the new hierarchy. This could not be as easily done in stone.

"Become the change you want the world to be."

Mahatma Gandhi

Chapter 11

OPEN MIND

"I have a friend who half believes in God. He does not believe in the existence of Spirit, soul, or energy bodies and believes that we are no more than bodies and mind. As to the Spirit question, he emphasizes lack of proof. Do you have something that you could say which might open his thinking a bit? I have mentioned Einstein and Stephen Hawking in their sense of God and the universe. I have talked about the common realm believed accessed by deep meditators. I have asked if he felt that the lives of Gandhi and the Dalai Lama are delusional. None of this has him even reconsidering."

We do not have to look very far back in history to see that proof did not always accompany theory, which later became unqualified acceptance. Bruno was burned at the stake for his views of the Earth not being the center of the known universe, and it was relatively recent that humanity believed that the Earth was flat. More recently it was proposed that there were particles and forces smaller than the atom. Of course all of these have become common scientific knowledge accepted by everyone.

In reference to your friend, we don't have to be spiritual about this or need to convince anyone of a truth. We just have to hold an open mind, saying simply that what was inconceivable twenty, fifty, or one hundred years ago is now common knowledge. So it is with the Spirit, the soul, and energy bodies, all of which exist and will be proven by science in the near future. Dr. Amit Goswami, a theoretical physicist, has written a book, *Physics of the Soul*, to prove the existence of the soul, and there are thousands of accounts of children remembering their past lives under experimental conditions.

Our own fabulous life is the greatest influence we can have on another person. Words are often used to convince others of our own beliefs, but the action in life of one's philosophy is far more powerful. There is nothing more contagious and compelling than a person who is passionate about something and gives up everything to pursue it.

"I would love for someone to help me decipher this dream I have had twice, the first time asleep, the second time awake. I seem to be traveling through space, going through wormholes and such. Then I slow down and come into a field of stars and finally stop. I look around and take in the scenery when my attention is drawn to my right. I notice a silhouette filled with stars (smaller and more compact) and this makes it easier for me to see her. She is in a kneeling position. To her left is someone who is lying down and then lifts their arm and turns the palm up. Soon a reddish-orange radiating ball of light starts traveling from the shoulder down the arm and into the palm of the hand. The other figure reaches out, levitates the ball into her hand, focuses, and then gently tosses the ball up into the universe. This process happens seven times in the exact same way. I recently had a reading inquiring who my guides were, what they could help me with, etc. I was warned about my health and was told that if I began healing my body great things would start to happen. I took the advice and started healing my body. (This reading happened on January 3, 2005.) I found RSE in four weeks and I am attending the beginner's class in Santa Fe in March. Are my spirit guides parts of me or are there guides that nudge us all?"

What an amazing dream! Most dreams, however dramatic, are the actions of the lower cerebellum to heal the body. This part of the brain will send images to the neocortex. The neocortex will then send signals to the parts of the body that need rejuvenation and cellular repair. It is consistent that this dream preceded those readings that warned you to heal your body.

I am, however, suspect to think that beings of divine intelligence (guides) would have an interest in answering our requests or, worse, be hanging around until we remember to make a request. Furthermore, is that what awaits evolved beings, to be assigned to an ignorant human being and "guide" them in their choices? People depend on guides when they are still ignorant and they do not know that what lies within each human being is the intelligence of the mind of God. Those who need guides as a way of elevating themselves are those who are poor in Spirit. Every human being comes prepackaged for greatness.

"Is RSE a cult?"

Many people have heard of RSE and they can find the organization through many avenues. The first thing people like to know is if it is a cult. I like Dr. Gordon Melton's definition of a cult. "It is a dirty little four-letter word you call someone you don't like." What is difficult to remember is that every mainstream religion was once called a cult by the reigning institution from which the upstart religious group was making a break. The original understanding of a cult originated from the word "occult," which meant hidden. In order to protect their vested interests, their congregation, and the offering basket passed each Sunday, they called these breakaway organizations by the derogatory term "cult."

If RSE can be described in one word, it would be that it is a school. It has a schedule of events, a curriculum for each class, and a variety of teachers, the main two being Ramtha and JZ Knight. In addition, its curriculum is vast in scope. A typical lecture may contain information from the disciplines of philosophy, theology, neuroscience, quantum physics, and neurobiology, to name a few. The school is a campus located in the midst of many acres of land and forest. It contains a bookstore, meeting hall, outdoor fields for practicing the techniques to develop the skills of focus, and a food court. It has many elements of a typical school campus.

The student population is highly educated with twenty percent of the students having a master's degree or higher. The median age is forty-one years old. Students come from all walks of life and from locations around the world. The school is located in the outskirts of a small town with less than 4,000 population, and at the same time the town has become an international setting with small businesses reflecting the many diverse cultures. It is an unusual town for such a small rural community.

RSE would seem strange to an outsider who did not have the knowledge of how we do phenomena at the school. If someone looked over the fence into one of the outside fields and saw a student levitate, they would probably be frightened and think that it was the work of the devil or an evil source that was actually taking over the body. However, if you went to an engineer and said that what you were doing was rotating the electromagnetic fields of energy around the body and spinning them sufficiently in a counterrotation to create an antigravity field effect, the engineer might say, "Yes that's how we do it with technology." RSE is a place where students practice manipulating the body with their minds within the laws of exotic physics. There has been no technology created that was greater than the mind that created it. Furthermore, according to Ramtha, technology has duplicated the workings of the human body to create antigravity devices, time machines, and other exotic technology. All technology is reverse-engineered from human capabilities. The great competition for harnessing zero- point energy is a field that is within the reach of every human being. Students who attend their first Beginning Retreat at our school learn how to do this.

"When you say that great minds were burned at the stake for heretical ideas that were eventually accepted by everyone, why haven't we learned from the past?"

Because the same organizations are still holding onto their investments regardless of what truths are being suppressed. That is how low humanity has become.

"We have heard of flying yogis, so they seem to exist."

Yes, but they do not threaten any organization because they are far removed from most people's perception. When you have a school, a public organization that is demonstrating these skills, then you can pose a threat. Most of the controversial press that has come out about the school is designed to discredit its credibility because it does threaten the established factions that can only survive if their masses stay ignorant. The greatest fear of those institutions is that there is a plausible explanation for this phenomena based on scientific principles. That information would completely undermine the church and its power over common people. This is the revolution that is starting to happen.

"Isn't the church concerned that individuals who develop these powers will misuse them for their own gain?"

That would be the thinking of an organization that is utilizing that precise strategy. There is an enormous transformation that must be made in order to develop these skills. By the time you have become a master at levitation or invisibility, you would have developed a mind that has no use for the misuse of power. When an individual is rich in the experience of life, they are not prone to wanting anything from anyone else. It isn't the phenomenon that is compelling. It is the journey in developing the phenomena that breeds the passion to use the skill as a springboard for further development. That is making known the unknown, the true spiritual journey.

"It is remarkable that there are relatively few people who come to the school, given what is being offered."

Most of the great teachers had small audiences. Most of the great teachers were far ahead of the philosophers and the scientists. Their radical message was controversial and the small audiences were in danger from the established organizations. While this condition is not as obvious today, the greatest deterrent to coming to our school is people's fear of changing their lives. That is the contemporary danger and the reason for relatively small audiences.

The beauty of our God is that we get to make any choice we want without regret or fear of retribution. We are continuously interacting with the quantum field and it is simply organizing our thoughts into a coherent, tangible reality. It is the working of an unconditional mind. It is our God. All of us are not sharing the same reality. The quantum field allows for all realities individually. What determines what we think and expect is the information we gain and accept during our lifetime. This is the only fundamental difference between people and how each person will create reality. Knowledge is so important. Imagine the difference in experience between one person who believes in heaven and hell, the one-life theory, and another person who understands the God within and the journey of discovery through incarnation. Each will get what they expect, for that is how the quantum field organizes those attitudes. If one's thoughts do create reality, as it is known in science, and what one believes determines one's experience in life, why not believe exactly what you want to experience? It makes absolutely no difference to your God, that Observer that continuously empowers your thoughts into the landscape of your life.

The reason why we are divine is because we have the mechanism to dream a dream and through our Observer to collapse that potential into tangible reality. While we are doing this all the time, with knowledge we have the freedom to do it consciously at any time.

"I was concerned when I heard that the school taught quantum physics because I didn't think I had the brain to understand it."

The quantum physics that is taught at the school is application specific. In other words, it is taught so that the concepts can be applied to improve the quality of your life. All of the science that is taught is to erase one's doubt so that the knowledge can be applied seamlessly to your life. For example, JZ Knight was able to heal herself of a terminal illness and she did it in one moment. She accomplished this because of her knowledge of the brain, its capabilities, and her love and understanding of quantum physics. Her accomplishment became the knowledge that was then formally taught to the students entitled the Neighborhood Walk^{SM}. It has become the platform of knowledge that has contributed to a whole host of miracles within the student body.

"How does mind over matter work?"

It would be wiser to say mind as matter. We are always going to be frequency specific with the people, places, things, times, and events in our lives. If we accept the concept that we are divine, with the innate ability and mandate to make known the unknown through manifested thought, then we must conclude that everything in our environment has our creative signature that we call frequency specific. If we take it one more step, we know that experience produces mind, so everything in our environment is our mind. Therefore mind is matter.

What is so remarkable about this understanding is that we do not have to travel to some high mountainous region to get feedback. We can see that within our own experience is the totality of our mind. If we want to change what we see, we know how to do that. This is an efficient and accessible feedback system.

"Do you have any recommendations on how to master

the out-of-body disciplines? Once we are out of the body is there a place we can go that is not limited by our own brain expectations?"

Every dream starts with the desire to experience that dream. If you hold that intent long enough, you will have its experience. Then you take your experience and expand it to include an even greater experience. Your interest in continually adding dimension and expansion to each subsequent experience will be the foundation of mastering the out-of-body experience. Each adventure will press the boundaries of the brain's expectation and limits. The brain is sensitive to and concerned with new frontiers of experience. As we have already learned, any potential experience that we desire that may have an unpredictable impact on our current reality is of concern to the neocortex. However, in knowing this we can expand our experience with each new adventure. If you moved up to the ceiling in your last experience and were concerned that you might bump your head, this time you go right through. The moment you venture into a territory that is not familiar, you have ventured beyond your brain's knowledge and its expectation. You are now free, and these new experiences will all be expansions beyond your brain's expectation.

"What about those people who have scary experiences?"

The scary experiences are a function of the neocortex tracking the out-of-body experience and becoming frightened because consciousness has left the body. Because the brain thinks the body is going to die, it panics, and consciousness is slammed back into the physical body often accompanied with a rapid heartbeat. It is very confusing and frightening. The other frightening experience is the infrared realm that houses the entities who left this plane with heavy habits or no knowledge of an afterlife and continue to cling to their earthbound experiences. These are the ghosts and apparitions that we occasionally see.

"I hear about your Holy Spirit, your God, the Observer, body/mind consciousness, being God, the traveler, personality, the ego, etc. Can you clarify what's what? Is it all in me? Which part thinks, observes, and creates? Is it all mind?"

Wow! Here is spirituality 101 in the next three minutes. It is all mind! Body/mind consciousness is the awareness and identification with our body. We behave as if we are our body and its needs rather than the Spirit that animates and is housed in the body. The consciousness and energy that is associated with the body always holds its physical needs as a priority. In the Great Work this level of awareness is one of the distractions that keeps each of us from making changes. Our God and the Observer is the same concept. God is a more religious and spiritual term, while the Observer is a term for both ancient philosophy and contemporary science. However, their function is the same. They endorse our thoughts into reality. The traveler is our Spirit. We are all eternal travelers in space and time. We are housed in different bodies according to the specific incarnation and the level of mind in which we are occupied. The personality, which is indigenous to each incarnation, is housed in the brain as a neurological network of attitudes. These are programs that we execute in order to survive in an environment. This personality is programmed by the soul, and the genetic body is predisposed to certain emotions that are yet to be owned into wisdom. Owning these predictable personality traits is the path of evolution. The word "ego" is most often associated with the personality. However, I have heard Ramtha say that ego is God. According to Ramtha it is the altered ego that is associated with the limitations of the personality.

"You mention runners. Do we not have them in our daily lives with our spiritual guides? I have not heard of spiritual guides in any of your archived interviews."

Runners are opportunities of divine intervention that create an experience that will give you insight. They are orchestrated by hierophants who have the power to send them. Ramtha is especially effective in doing this. You will not hear much about spiritual guides because we do not use them. We depend upon the God within for our guidance. I especially like Ramtha's thoughts on spiritual guides. He asks why one might think that all an evolved spiritual being has to do is "sit around" and be available for our boring questions and if that is what the afterlife has to offer us, it has been poorly designed. To know who you are means to be responsible for the divinity that we are. To depend on anything outside of ourselves is to be afraid to claim that legacy.

"What is enlightenment?"

Enlightenment means "in knowledge of." What is the knowledge? The knowledge is to be able to answer the four great questions and to know that you are the Observer in a field of infinite potentials and whatsoever you observe becomes the landscape and the experience of your life. This concept merits being repeated so that it will become hardwired in the brain. If you repeat something enough it will become part of one's long-term memory.

"Do you believe the original sin caused humans to become separate in the Garden of Eden and from God?"

To answer the question we must ask the question about the original sin. Are we talking about Eve having eaten of the fruit of knowledge? There were hosts of humanity before Adam and Eve, so the word "original" in this context makes no sense. Furthermore, why was knowledge considered a sin? The original definition of sin was "to miss the mark." It was a term used by archers when they did not hit their target. Somehow the word "sin" came to be defined as a transgression against God. This was a convenient translation that helped the church hold onto its constituents, as any transgression against God was considered wrong. It has always fascinated me that the Bible was not translated into English for thirteen centuries after the life of Jesus. Can you imagine how many times it has been rewritten and translated to give us the current editions?

In the Schools of Ancient Wisdom there is only experience and learning, so you cannot have sin, original or otherwise. There never was an original sin. According to Ramtha, the Garden of Eden was a laboratory for enhancing primitive man through the splicing of genetic materials from a superior race. We are the products of those laboratory experiments. You can never become separated from what you are. As Gods, even though forgotten, we cannot be separate from ourselves. There is historical documentation that gives us a different picture from the one supported by religious organizations that are completely invested in the misinformation. If you read the Nag Hammadi Library, discovered in 1945 in Egypt, you will read a vastly different description of the life of Jesus and his message. Zecharia Sitchen's work in the *Earth Chronicles* and Michael Cremo's *Forbidden Archeology* are two books that will expand your mind beyond what is conventionally accepted. However, the best account of the history of humanity is Ramtha's teachings in a two-volume set called *A Master's Reflection on the History of Humanity*, Parts 1 & 2. These documents will enlighten and educate you beyond what is readily available.

"I never believed in hell but wondered where the Lucifer story originated. There are some stories about an ancient race, the destruction of their planet, and the need to be banished to Earth as a punishment. Has Ramtha mentioned this?"

Ramtha has mentioned the name Lucifer in reference to a planet with that name. It makes historical sense that Lucifer would have "fallen" or been banished from its home and relegated to the Earth. Of course religious organizations will use a thin thread of this ancient knowledge to insist that Lucifer, the devil, was banished from heaven by God and placed on

Earth to tempt the hearts and minds of honest men. Ramtha's view of history and his vision of the cosmos over the past 35,000 years continue to give us the best reference as to how these stories were interpreted, recorded, and communicated to fulfill the agenda of organizations and their need for power and control.

"A friend who has studied Scientology has a different meaning than how Ramtha has taught about mind. Would you give a brief understanding of mind?"

It's a great question because it requires knowing the difference between consciousness, the brain, and mind. Consciousness is a river of thought that is always accessible to us. Once a thought is isolated from this river and contemplated upon, using the brain, it produces a by-product called mind. So consciousness and its action on the brain produces mind. In other words, the brain processes consciousness to produce mind. The quality of mind is what produces the quality of life. It is the template in which all of our experiences manifest. If we can learn to change our mind, we will create a different life with different experiences. Students in the school continuously focus on new concepts from the river of consciousness that will add to the knowledge base and to the experience of their lives. The greater our contemplations become, the greater the mind that is produced, and that gives us an expanded reality.

When we understand the relationship of mind to our environment, we realize that it is not mind over matter that we are able to accomplish but rather the understanding that mind is matter. It is out of our mind, the culmination of contemplations from the river of consciousness, that we produce the people, places, things, times, and events in our life. The mind becomes a template for the experiences of our life. The reason knowledge is so important is that it allows us to build greater models of thought. Those models of thought, once focused upon, add to our mind, which produces these greater realities.

"We lead our lives like water
flowing down a hill,
going more or less in one direction
until we splash into something
that forces us to find a new course."

Memoirs of a Geisha

Chapter 12

EMOTIONS

"I've been studying Ramtha's teachings for seventeen years and I'm finally attending my first Beginning Retreat this fall, which I'm quite thrilled about. In Ramtha's older teachings he used to say that emotion was the prize of creation and the very reason for life. Now he seems to be saying that we should be free of our emotion. Could you please explain this seeming incongruity?"

This is a fabulous question. If you can understand my response you will be one of the few people, along with the students of the school, who understand emotion and its place in creation.

Emotion is the prize of creation and the very reason for life on this level of reality. We are living in a three-dimensional reality. In making known the unknown, the only law of God, we create a dream for the specific reason to have its experience. Our experience is emotion, the prize of creation. This process of dreaming, experiencing, and then building a bigger dream based on the former experiences of creation is how we evolve. This is the divine instruction from God.

Human beings have not been well taught by those in leadership. We understand that an old regime in power (organized religion) does not easily give up its base of influence. When these teachings say that we are to be free of emotions, we are talking about the predictable behaviors (habits) that are used for emotion only. When we get caught in an emotional loop, a habit, or a neuronet (as it is called in science), that predictable behavior guarantees that we respond to situations or similar situations with the same emotional response. These teachings say that we need to be free from predictable and repetitive responses of emotion .

The emotions of fear, anger, jealousy, doubt, unworthiness, and any response that always accompanies certain circumstances or situations are the emotions that need to be owned and resolved into wisdom. This is the work of the true spiritual journey.

Here is the great distinction that needs to be made regarding the use of emotions in the creative process. When dreaming a dream so as to bring that reality into your life, you will never create a new experience if that dream is accompanied with emotion. We know this because emotion is the prize or end product of an experience. If we use emotion in the creative process, we will create a reality we have already had because the emotion that is being used with the new dream will always equate to a former experience from the past. This new dream will be a repeat of a former experience. This is why relationships always end up the same even though the players seem to have changed.

When creating a new idea, you must visualize that idea without emotion. The way this is accomplished is by taking an image of the idea and holding it in concentrated focus until consciousness moves into the parts of the brain that are without emotion. When this reality manifests, it will not have any association to your past because it will not have been accompanied with any emotion. All emotions are associated with a past experience.

"All humans are pretty much emotional and are masking some kind of fear. What is it that you think humans fear the most?"

Death is what all humans fear the most. All other fears are simply variations on this theme. To overcome one's fear of death would catapult any person on a spiritual path. This was Ramtha's suggestion to Yeshua ben Joseph, that he confront death head-on. This was Yeshua's last great initiation, which led him to be able to resurrect himself from the dead. Resurrection is the last initiation of a Christ.

As we have been told several times by our teacher, no one can become immortal while still fearing death. It would mean that one's focus is on their body rather than the essence that animates the body. The moment you put your awareness on your Spirit, you become aware of that ancient, eternal being. It is difficult to really live a free and expanded life when so many choices are influenced by our fear of death.

The fear of death is a cancer to humanity. The greatest proponents of this fear are the religions that need that propaganda as a basis of reality in order to control their flock. This is the greatest sin that has been perpetrated upon humanity, and it is perpetrated by the very organizations that claim to have the answer to salvation. Ramtha has told us that there is a place in the infrared realm that, for as far as the eye can see, people are dead in Christ and in suspended animation waiting for his return. This is an example of the justice of the quantum field and how it organizes itself into realities that are believed. Even masters who have passage to those levels of reality find it a near-impossible task to wake them from their conviction.

"Can knowledge replace fear and anger?"

It has to start with knowledge. Knowledge is the precursor to experience. When you realize who you are, where you have come from, what your destiny is, and how you go about completing that destiny, you begin to have experiences that will alleviate fear and eventually dissolve it.

"Why is there a reluctance to accept the concept that we are living as a hologram, subject to our thoughts and attitudes?"

Look at what must change. You would have to take responsibility for everything that happens to you. That works well when things are smooth or predictable, but the moment there is a crisis you immediately look to see who or what you can blame. The concept of victimization would disappear. To make this shift from victim to creator would catapult you immediately into power and the resources of mind to create fabulous realities. The very reason why there is reluctance is because you would have to give up the emotions and the habits that can be relied on in your current life. There is no power unless you acknowledge that you create reality and that you both celebrate and suffer the consequences of your choices. When you reach this level of understanding on a consistent basis, you will have the consistent power to live your life on your own self-created terms.

"The recent events with the earthquake and tsunami created a lot of change for some beings. Does the Earth create some events to get our attention?"

The Earth is a living organism and wants to live just like all organisms that struggle to survive. It will endeavor to shake off the ticks on its skin if they become an irritant. Humanity has become a disrespectful inhabitant of this environment.

The tsunami was a powerful runner in many respects. It brought out the greed in a government that valued profits over safety in not wanting to empty the hotels of their high-paying tourists. It showed the world how out-of-touch with nature most humanity is, as none of the wild animals or indigenous people were caught off guard. All of the animals, except the domestic breeds, went to higher ground before and after the first quake. The animals and the indigenous people operate from a different part of their brain than does civilized humanity. They sensed that there would be a second and more violent reaction to the quake. The tourists, on the other hand, were consumers without much interest in such primitive qualities and they paid a price for that arrogance.

As bad as the tsunami was and other cataclysmic events are,

such as the hurricanes that continue to pound the borders of the southern United States, global warming will be the most devastating. This melting of the ice sheets will be more globally dangerous than any isolated catastrophe. This is the result of pillaging the Earth and decades of favoring profits over scientific evidence and warnings. Man has not been a good steward of the land for a long time, and the worst is yet to come. The tsunami was a warning that when your bottom line of financial well-being is more important than your health or that of the home you inhabit, you will eventually be engulfed by a similar big wave.

"Is being uncomfortable a part of being a student in the school?"

One day when I asked the Webcast hosts (both students in the RSE School) how they were doing, they replied, "Well, we've been a little uncomfortable since that last event several weeks ago." I laughed out loud as I told them that I had been uncomfortable for twenty-three years. Being uncomfortable is a consistent experience with anyone who is in the midst of change. Being uncomfortable means that you have pressed up against the walls of your own predictable comfort zone and you are choosing whether to continue to move into the new experience or retreat back to the familiar. Inside the walls of our neuronet we are comfortable and highly predictable while everything else is uncertain and uncomfortable. As a student in the Great Work, you get used to being uncomfortable and yet remaining functional. When I helped people walk on fire as a discipline of mind over matter, the intent of the seminar was to empower individuals to be able to take action in the face of fear. This act of walking on fire would become a badge of courage for all of those times in your life when you could use the memory of a powerful experience to help you through a difficult circumstance. It is similar in our school. There are many times when we are uncomfortable and yet it does not stop us from pressing ourselves into a new experience. Being uncomfortable means that we are bridging into the unknown, and that is the path of evolution. However, what generally stops us from evolving into a new adventure is the preconceived conclusion that change always equates to loss. Change equates re-formation. We decide how we judge the outcome. An initiate sees it as evolution without judgment or conclusion.

"How can I differentiate between a state of depression and a state of a tired emotional body?"

With a little rest you can restore your tired emotional body. However, if you are depressed, that same amount of rest will not give you relief. A state of depression is the lack of personal expression. If you pay attention to your thoughts, you will know why you are depressed. Whoever or whatever you blame for your depressed circumstances will be your reasons for your depression. Now you think about it more because of how you feel, and those thoughts trigger more emotions and it becomes more difficult not to think about your depression. This will continue in a closed loop until you change the way you think. What is the secret to changing this? You must stop the loop of internal dialogue that triggers the emotions that must respond to those thoughts that make you feel depressed. The body is servant to the mind. Our job as students is to master our thoughts so that the body is given the proper directions.

If we use this example of depression in a broader context, we can look at every aspect of our life and know that it is a blueprint of our thinking. In any area in which we think our life does not match our expectations of ourself, we simply need to examine our thoughts in that area and change our thinking to correspond with that new dream of ourself. We have very effective disciplines in our school that we use to exact these kinds of changes.

"How does laziness factor into creation?"

It is one of the ways in which the neocortex expresses its objection to change. The neocortex is always going to object to change because it cannot predict the impact of the new circumstance on your current reality. Its job is to make sure you make choices that support the survival of the organism, which is your body. This part of the brain expresses itself as lethargy, confusion, doubt, fear, or any other emotion that will inhibit your interest in thinking about the new possibility. The three greatest distractions to a new creation are the environment, our body, and time. The environment will always show us the antithesis of what we are creating, and this leads to doubt. Our bodies will send the signals of boredom, pain, or frustration to get our attention, and time is everyone's nemesis.

As students we must be able to focus on a concept with such a degree of concentration that the internal picture of what it is we want to create is more real than those three distractions that battle for out attention. This and its refinements are the ultimate keys to the kingdom of heaven.

"Other teachers have said that the most important ingredient in creating something is putting as much emotion into that creation as you can. The more emotions you can put into it, the quicker the manifestation. This seems contradictory to Ramtha's teachings on manifesting without emotions, but this is much easier for me to do. Can you explain?"

If you use emotions in creating a new reality, it will not be a new reality when it manifests. Emotions are the end product of a created experience. Any emotions you would use would be from a past experience. It is easier because it is familiar and has an emotional reference. It is much more difficult to create an abstract and unknown concept without an emotional reference. Ramtha asks us to focus on something we want to create or experience without emotions so that the new reality is without a past reference. How can we put an emotion on something that we have yet to experience? The emotions will be the end product of the new experience. If you want a new experience, it must be created without the familiar emotions of the past.

This is accomplished by presenting the new idea to the Observer that is without judgment, conclusion, or emotion.

"My mother passed away a few years ago and I am suffering from anxiety and depression since her passing. What happens after death? Will I see my mother again and recognize her? How can I get over the guilt of my past?"

You suffer from anxiety and depression because you do not have the knowledge or the answers to the questions you have asked. Death is a transition from one dimension of reality into another, more glorious dimension. You and I have made this transition tens of thousands of times. When your mother passed from this dimension she was drawn into a tunnel and rapidly journeyed to a wall of light. At the light she was met by her loved ones that she easily recognized. She had a light review in which she watched her entire life, from conception to her passing, and how she reacted to those experiences in her life. She then watched it again, only this time she saw how each of her decisions, reactions, and choices affected the people around her. This is the most painful part of the review, but this will show her what she has yet to own as wisdom in the experience of becoming a transcendent human being. With this new understanding she would have the opportunity to contemplate her life and how she wants to design the next experience that will optimize her chances of evolving. When she is ready, her God and her soul will arrange for an incarnation and place her into the most appropriate genetic body that will compel her to confront those same unresolved issues that define her as a human being. And the process continues.

When you realize that your guilt and your anxiety are the very genetic propensities that you have returned with, you might be more conscious and interested in owning those experiences so that you can evolve without having to have another light review. Emotional responses that always occur to the same or similar circumstances are considered habits, and these are the emotions that must be owned in order to evolve spiritually. Our parents are not people we have lived with lifetime after lifetime that would create an allegiance and a loyalty to them. They are the providers of the specific genetic material that is necessary to continue our evolutionary journey. Furthermore, once we are out of this emotional body, there is no guilt, shame, or regret regarding our life and those involved in it. With this perspective it might become easier to relieve the guilt that is often associated with our relationship to our parents.

"I know that emotions are chemical and that the addiction to those chemicals is responsible for disease, aging, and finally death. What about joy and happiness? Are they emotions with chemicals that add to disease?"

This is a great question and deserves clarification. The emotions that lead to cellular mutation that eventually begins the slow demise of the body are those emotions of limitation. If we continue to respond to the circumstances in our life with the same predictable emotional responses, there is a definite effect on the body. We call these habits. Habits over time do the same damage to our body as a record that is continuously played in the same groove. Eventually the record will break down from overuse. Some of the emotions that lead to the breakdown of the body are fear, anger, envy, jealousy, insecurity, frustration, unworthiness, doubt, greed, and any other emotion that is an automatic response to a specific circumstance.

Happiness and joy are the natural states of a being who lives without habits. The chemical effect and subsequent emotions are rejuvenating to the body. Happiness is the result of having new adventures and developing the courage to change your life to take advantage of new opportunities. If we learned to live more like children, who know the secret of being in the present moment, we would become slow to age, immune to disease, and live a long, extended life.

"A concept that is not dangerous
can hardly be called a concept at all."

Oscar Wilde

Chapter 13

THE BRAIN

"What about the things that I want to change that do not change? If I am so powerful, why does this happen?"

You are not using the brain properly. Instead of creating a new reality, you are using the same mind-set to try to create something new, and this will not deliver the new reality. It will deliver the same old reality because the same mind-set is doing the creating. If we use the example of the sun as our God (Observer) and the stained-glass windows (neuronet, attitude) as our mind-set, no matter what you want to see reflected on the cathedral floor (reality), the reflection will always be in the pattern of the stained-glass window (attitude).

When someone says, "You know, I really want this but I don't seem to be able to bring it about," there is another very good reason why this happens. The very part of the brain that helps us imagine what it would be like to experience this is the same part of the brain that also needs to know what impact this reality is going to have on our current life. If this part of the brain cannot be certain as to the impact of this new reality, it is going to have a psychological objection to its creation. The part of the brain that helps us create reality is also the part of the brain that has the greatest objection to uncertain new realities. This is the classic definition of a conflict of interest. We use the neocortex to design the concept of what it is we want to create or experience. We do this by creating a visual drawing or symbol that represents what we want. When we begin to focus on this visual, if we do not anesthetize this part of the brain and its objections we will be distracted and not have the focus necessary to create this new reality.

"In my understanding we have seven bodies that are aligned with different parts of our brain. Do you believe that the specific frequencies of all seven bodies can be latent in the unused or untapped areas of our brain?"

We know that anything another person has experienced is a potential for anyone else to experience. We all come prepackaged with the same equipment, and all of the experiences recorded to date can be called the mind of God. So if someone has levitated, they have used their brain, their will, and their imagination to do this. The mechanics of creating any reality is the same process. Therefore there is a place in the brain that if occupied can be the map for any experience. These areas in the brain are latent and can be activated by understanding knowledge and being trained in the process of creating reality.

Knowledge is the road map. Without a road map it is difficult to find one's destination. It is easier now to understand that without knowledge, humanity will continue to use less than ten percent of their brain.

"What is the science of doubt? What is the science of acceptance? Does it take a greater mind to accept than it does to doubt?"

The science is the same. If certain information falls far outside of our accepted reality, then there is an immediate reaction of doubt. If on the other hand the information falls within our accepted reality, then it is easily accepted. Depending on our experience we will either doubt or accept all new information. If you are referring to a greater mind in relation to greater realities, then those concepts not normally accepted by conventional thought do take a greater mind for acceptance than for doubt. Human beings are skeptical by nature because most unconventional thought if accepted would have a great impact on one's life and we know that this is not acceptable in most cases. There are countless examples of what conventional thought doubted several hundred years ago that is now unanimously accepted.

"Why does being still and quiet allow us to receive great answers and great understandings?"

When we become quiet and still we relax the part of the brain that is the most active, keeping a steady watch on the environment in order to make a quick decision if necessary. Once the neocortex is still, awareness moves to another part of the brain that has access to greater knowledge. These deeper realms of the mind contain vastly different information than the neocortex, the guardian of our reality. The information that can be accessed in these deeper levels of mind rarely surfaces while the neocortex is active. In our school we have often heard Ramtha say, "Be still and know that you are God." That is an accurate statement, and we have disciplines that develop this skill.

"Can people achieve this without discipline?"

Yes, but it is more difficult and time-consuming because knowledge is the map and without knowledge it can be hit-and- miss to find your chosen location. The disciplines are used to prepare the brain for extraordinary results. We practice disciplines to the point that they become part of our mind-set. Then the experience is only a thought away. Some forms of meditation can give you this state of stillness. Most of us have felt a great sense of peace while immersed in nature, sitting by a lake, or observing a stunning sunrise. However, it is what you become in this stillness that allows for greater realities to be created and then experienced.

A walk in the woods or a stroll by a river will have an effect on your thinking. The frequency of nature is of a higher order than social consciousness, and you will think different thoughts than those you think in your home or work environment. You will access a different part of the brain in nature than you do in a more social environment. All environments are frequency specific. All frequency carries information. The information you will be receiving in nature will be vastly different from the information the city has to offer. And isn't it interesting that busy people who have lots of things to take care of rarely find the time to be in nature. It is because they are frequency specific with their busier environment.

In manifesting new realities the concept of acceptance is a really big key. Without acceptance, people who say they are going to manifest a gold bar in their hand or levitate find that it doesn't work. If someone is trying or desiring to create a new reality — any new reality — it cannot happen through trying or desiring. What you will experience every time is trying and desiring. What you must do is become the gold bar or the one who can levitate. Once you become it, you will move consciousness to the part of the brain that has this capability, and the Observer will be looking through a neuronet that can execute this experience. Remember, we have the same brain that is shared by six billion other human beings on this planet. Therefore if any person has had the experience that you are becoming, then you have the equipment necessary for that same experience. Is there anything you want or any experience you want to have that has not been accomplished by some other human being? Probably not!

"We hear that we use less than ten percent of our brain."

We do, but that statement that is so often used is misleading. The scientists never said how much less than ten percent we use. As it turns out with the latest findings, we use one to two percent of our brain's capacity. This percentage was established and correlated when the human genome was mapped, and it was discovered that we express 30,000 to 60,000 different genetic sequences, which equates to one or two percent of our DNA. So we as human beings use one to two percent of our brain and the same percentage of our potential DNA. Human beings are the very definition of underachievers.

"What is the other ninety-plus percent of our brain doing?"

It is waiting for someone intelligent to give it instructions. It is a testament that we have not reached the pinnacle of our human potential.

"In your interviews you have mentioned that the Consciousness & Energy[SM] **technique is used to anesthetize old programs and place new programs in the brain. How is this technique performed?"**

It is performed just as you have suggested. It is accomplished through the C&E® breath technique. This breath technique is performed to anesthetize the part of our brain that is always objecting to change. Specifically, it will object to any circumstance or situation that may threaten one's current reality, and that will be perceived as any new change in your life. However, once we anesthetize that part of the brain, a new concept can be introduced without objection. Once you learn how to focus on that new dream without distraction, you will have found the key to manifestation.

This breath technique is not similar to kundalini yoga and is not used to create the same outcome. The kundalini breath technique is a cleansing breath. The C&E® breath is used to allow consciousness to move into deeper levels of mind so that you can create extraordinary realities with the parts of the brain that can facilitate those new realities.

"It seems simple enough. What makes it so hard to do?"

The process is easy. What makes it difficult is each of us

being willing to make changes in our life without knowing exactly how those changes will come about and what the end result will be once those changes are integrated into our new life. It takes courage in the beginning to make those initial changes because we have the attitude that change is loss. Once we make small changes and survive those changes, we realize the benefits of that process and we begin to see change as gain. Once that is accomplished, we become much more willing and even eager to change. Now we are on a march in evolution and fulfilling the only law of God, to make known the unknown.

In our school most students eventually learn that unless we are threatening our comfort zone, change is not happening as an evolutionary process. We have learned that if we continue to experience the past, which means the same predictable emotions over and over, the cells of our body will not receive any new information, and like a record that is played over and over the groove will eventually get so deep that it will no longer be able to play the tune. Not changing, which means that no new information is getting to the cells, is what wears the body out. Aging is directly correlated to repetitious, predictable behavior. Therefore youth and longevity are correlated to change.

"How do we interrupt or break old thought patterns and replace them with new ones? Sometimes old thoughts creep in during the day. I want to stay aligned with the new thought that I am creating for myself. How do we maintain it through the day? Some call it mind chatter. I want my new thoughts to be the dominant thoughts."

If you have completed the Beginner's Retreat, you know that you must create your day and that at any point during the day you begin to hear that mind chatter you must go for a Neighborhood Walk[SM] to reinforce the new thoughts.

If you have not participated in one of our Retreats, then here is what you can do. The moment the old thoughts begin to creep in as mind chatter, you must simply observe them from a detached point of view, as if you were watching someone else's thoughts. If you do this successfully, you will not engage the emotional loop that is attached to this thought pattern. All thoughts are attached to an emotion. If you can become detached with this same thought pattern, then that thought pattern will disconnect itself neurologically. Once it is detached neurologically, it cannot fire as a thought and you will never have that specific mind chatter again. If you continue to do this, you will eventually retire all of the old thought patterns and you will become a radically different and enlightened person. This simple process engages the original and only mandate from God, and that is to make known the unknown. Retiring mind chatter is the ultimate path in evolution, for you are retiring the emotions that accompany those thoughts. The ramifications of this are enormous. Emotions wear out the body. If you retire the emotions, you extend your biological life. If you get really good at this, you will live long enough to see immortality as a viable life science.

"What is the aim of a master student? Is it to clean the neocortex of all limited attitudes, replace them with unlimited thoughts, and with the help of the midbrain and the reptilian brain to live your entire life from the midbrain without having to access anything from the neocortex?"

The aim of the sincere students in our school is to conquer ourselves, to master the need of reacting to our environment with limited, predictable emotional responses. Every time we do that we are fulfilling the only law of God.

The absence of using the neocortex is not an aim or a desire. It provides us with a very important function. The neocortex, by sending us messages that we interpret as voices, will constantly insist that we make choices that support the survival of our body. It is going to remind us to look both ways before crossing the street and to take a step or two back from the cliff while enjoying the view. We would not be able to make these same distinctions in the midbrain and we would be placing ourselves in physical risk. The neocortex constantly assesses the environment and creates potential strategies for survival, so we do not want to abandon this part of our brain.

The neocortex is the part of our brain in which we design the picture of what it is we want to create. It is eminently important. The midbrain is used to change the past and to know the future, while the reptilian brain, also called the cerebellum, is used to observe any thought into reality. In any manifestation process we refer to the architect as the neocortex, the builder as the cerebellum, and together they provide the hardware for creating reality.

"I am one of four young men who attended your consciousness and energy workshop in the mountains of Austria. I still remember one sentence you said after we finished our C&E® session. "You look beautiful. Manifestation will come quickly." Meanwhile, six months later I am still doing my C&E® and blowing with passion and waiting for my manifestations. I am working on getting rid of my doubts, my frustration, and to create enough money to attend all RSE events. I want my subconscious mind to create extraordinary manifestations. And just lately I am hearing the voices that are trying to convince me to stop the work because it is not working."

These are typical concerns and important to every new student. First of all, it is not my consciousness and energy workshop. It is Ramtha's teachings and disciplines. I am honored to have been appointed to facilitate them. It is not your subconscious mind that creates anything. It is your subconscious mind that is connected to the quantum field of all potentials. More importantly, when the voices begin to talk to you it is a sign that you are at the end of the battle and victory is near. The voices are the product of the existing neuronet, and it knows that change is imminent. It is putting forth its best effort to stifle that change. As Ramtha has told us many times, the intensity of the battle is the greatest just before the end, so the voices represent that the end is at hand. This is the point at which many students give up. They succumb to the voices. However, you now know that victory is at hand. Congratulations. All you have to do at this point is commit yourself to the outcomes that you have stated regardless of how long it takes. That attitude transcends time, and the Observer will simply override the objections and endorse these desires into reality.

"Can you tell me about DNA and the ascension process? There are people who claim they can activate twelve or twenty-two or however many strands of DNA that are latent in us. How can they do this? How can we do it on our own?"

There is so much misinformation about the DNA strands. Several years ago the scientists who were mapping the human genome discovered that human beings express 30,000 to 60,000 different combinations of genetic sequence. I think it is important to know that this represents an activation of only one to two percent of the potential standard, double-helix DNA. So why would someone claim to be able to activate twelve strands? They would make those claims so that it would appear that they were special. If any individual even expressed ten percent of their DNA potential, they would be so extraordinary that they would not have to make such ridiculous claims. They would be able to demonstrate their masterful abilities. I have yet to see any such demonstration by anyone making such claims. We are hard-pressed to express more than the 60,000 combinations, and I find it premature that someone is talking about twelve and twenty-two strands of DNA. It is this kind of ignorance that gives the New Age such a bad reputation.

Every human being has the necessary DNA to accomplish any task they can imagine. Therefore in the simplest of terms, whatever has been accomplished by any human being, past, present, or future, had to express the necessary DNA to accomplish that task. The masters of the Far East, Apollonius of Tyana, and Ramtha the Enlightened One are examples of extraordinary individuals who utilized combinations of genes to accomplish legendary feats. If they did the things that they are reported to have done, then that same DNA sequence is available in you and me. It is not important to listen to someone who talks about the activation of numerous strands of DNA if they cannot express these additional strands themselves. It is important, however, to listen to those who have accomplished and can demonstrate those very acts of extraordinary ability.

In conclusion, if anyone has ascended, then that same activation of the DNA that raises the frequency in the body to that level exists for all of us. If you have been taught how to take a two-dimensional drawing and focus it into a three-dimensional hologram, then you know the secret to the ascension process.

"Why do people's cloaks go invisible when they do? Do people know they are going invisible when it happens?"

The clothing is within the electromagnetic fields of frequencies that surround the body and are subject to the same laws. An object or body becomes invisible when its rate of frequency is fast enough that the human eye cannot see it. This is similar to the blades of a household fan turned up to "high." You can feel the wind but you cannot see the blades. The clothing becomes invisible because it is a part of that faster frequency.

In the beginning people do not know they are becoming invisible. When I levitated in the name-field with my eyes open, I did not know what had happened until I felt one foot on the ground and then the next foot that followed. During the levitation I saw nothing until my second foot hit the ground and then my vision returned. I asked Ramtha why I had no conscious awareness of this experience. He explained that the part of the brain that was facilitating this experience was not sufficiently developed for me to be consciously aware of it but that I could develop my awareness by repeating the experience. We become aware of these abilities as we are able to repeat them.

One of our students was working on bilocation at her house. She had her blinders on and suddenly saw an injured bird on her porch and her cat about ready to jump on it. The next thing she realized was that she was holding the bird in her hands on the deck of her front porch. Without thinking, she tried to get back into her house. It was locked with a deadbolt from the inside. She lives alone and only at this point did she begin to realize what had happened. She was in her bathrobe and walked to her barn to get the extra set of keys. She had bilocated through the walls of her house to rescue an injured bird. She was horrified that she was still in her nightgown. She vowed from that day on that she would not work on bilocation unless she was fully dressed. Once again there was a lapse in conscious awareness during the bilocation experience. This student had remarkable skills that were witnessed by many students. However, she was caught cheating on a discipline several years later. Although there was no reason to doubt her story at the time she told it, a breach of trust at any point always casts a shodow of doubt in many directions.

Whatever is in your magnetic field during these phenomenal moments will be a part of that experience. When a person bilocates or levitates, the field is so strong that it affects those around it and those within it. There is dissolution of mass and a reorganization of that mass. I have heard that there is a museum of the famous tornadoes of Oklahoma that shows the effect of a torsion field on mass. In the museum there are glass mirrors with a straw penetrating the glass without damage to either object. Torsion physics and the counterrotating electromagnetic fields around the body are the sciences that substantiate the phenomena of bilocation and levitation.

"If we understand that the quantum field contains all possibilities, that they exist simultaneously, and that free will and choice dictates perception, then what is the nature of unconsciousness?"

Its nature is the unconscious intelligence of a neuronet or program that can be activated by a single thought. Walking is a program that is unconscious, which means you only have to think about it to activate its program. Most people do not think about digestion, filtering their blood, or maintaining a rhythmic heartbeat. These are additional examples of unconscious programs that display the nature and intelligence of unconsciousness.

"Why is it hard to hold onto a single holographic image?"

Because it goes against everything we have identified as ourselves. This image is already up against the objection of the part of the brain that is making decisions on our behalf and its survival. Holding this image as a concentrated focus is a battle between the old regime and the new. All it takes for a successful overthrow is to hold our focus of that image until the internal picture becomes more real than the distractions of our body, the environment, and time.

The personality is fearful that this new reality will be less useful than the old paradigm. During this transition there will be a short period of chaos. In biology this period is called perturbation. The observation in nature is that as an organism changes to adapt, it will always change itself into a more elegant and efficient organization. This is precisely what happens to people who make changes in their lives.

"How can we dissolve the power of the inner demons that use lots of life energy to keep us under control? Do these already exist in the mind? How do we observe the self at all times to dissolve those inner demons?"

Everything that we experience already exists in the mind. How you have created these inner demons is your business, but since you have asked, there is a way out. Every time you feel that you are under the control of these inner demons, your greatest strategy is to simply observe their interaction with you. As long as you do not respond to them with emotions, the by-product of thought, you will eventually atrophy their ability to interact with you. They are a neurological phenomena created by you and as such they can be dissolved as easily.

The moment that you interact with the thought, you reinforce the connection. However, if we observe the self during any unwanted behavior, we can master the thought that leads to that behavior. That is the path of mastery and of making known the unknown. Through repeated observation we can dissolve the neurological connections that are the forerunners to any emotional experience. You only need to do this a few times to break the connection.

"I wonder about programming the subconscious mind. Can childcare workers become unhappy by being programmed daily by unhappy children?"

The subconscious mind is programmed by repeated observations. If you practice anything long enough it will become subconscious and can be activated by a simple thought. For most of us the example of walking is a program that can be activated by the thought of wanting to get up and begin to walk. We can be programmed by anything we accept, including unhappy children. Anything we identify with can influence our behavior. However, we can exercise the power of detachment that allows us to observe circumstances without becoming a part of those circumstances. There is documentation that suggests that many medical professionals die of what it is they are attempting to heal in other people and the same holds true for actors that become their roles so convincingly that they often end up in similar circumstances. However, we always have a choice whether we accept that or not.

If we have the courage to look at this at a deeper level of understanding, we come to realize that the environment of unhappy children exists because it exists within us. Remember the doctor from Hawaii. If we change our mind, the environment must change to reflect that change of mind. You can have the most boring job, but if you meet someone and fall in love, the boring job becomes an adventure because you are now on an adventure. That is the power of changing your mind. It changes everything.

"Ramtha states that brain cells once destroyed do not regenerate. Recent research, however, has documented that they do regenerate. Can you comment?"

They can regenerate and Ramtha has known this all along. If you were the first human being born of flesh and blood to ascend, then you would know the power of mind as matter. His comments on destroying brain cells were in relationship to taking drugs. It is true that the latest research shows that brain cells can be regenerated in certain parts of the brain, and Ramtha would be the first to acknowledge this. However, the brain cells that are destroyed by drugs do not regenerate, and that would comply with the concept that attitudes have a direct effect on the body.

"Can you shed some light on Alzheimer's disease? I am a nurse and it is difficult for me to see purposeful good in this disease. Why would Spirit preserve their life when they seem helpless to help themselves?"

Alzheimer's is becoming epidemic because people are not doing anything new. They continue the same thinking patterns to the point that those patterns crystallize. Now we have a person who cannot fire the neuronets of recognition or remembrance. With this the Holy Spirit and the soul realize that this person is not going to learn anything new and they begin the process of the demise of the body. The heavy metals in the bloodstream are reflective of the rigid, nonflexible thinking patterns of these individuals. Remember the slogan, "As within, so without."

In *USA Today*, August 18, 2005, the research showed that people who were retiring had financial savings accounts but were without cognitive savings accounts. This recent research showed that there was a methodology for inhibiting the onset of these neurodegenerative diseases. Walking was the best form of exercise to keep the brain young. It actually birthed new brain cells. The article went on to stipulate that learning something new or exercising the brain with activities like crossword puzzles also kept those diseases at bay. In essence we have a simple strategy for preventing neurodegenerative diseases.

In addition, we use this understanding to enhance the discipline of our Neighborhood Walk^{SM}. If you can combine walking, which produces new brain cells, with the statements of who you have always been, you are creating new frequency specific brain cells that will program a reality that will have an immediate effect on your life.

"Where in the brain do obsessions arise?"

All obsessions are housed in the neocortex. They are a product of the genetics that we inherit from our parents. They are absolutely necessary because they are what we have yet to own. All obsessions are crying out for help and want to be owned into wisdom and retired. We do this by observing the circumstance that provokes the obsession rather than unconsciously responding. If we can do this consistently several times, we will atrophy the neurological connections that fire this behavior. This is how we own an obsession and evolve into a greater being. We are always in control of what we dismantle or create according to how we place our attention. Fear always manifests because fears are given so much attention and thought. The quickest way to get something is to be afraid that you will get it. It is almost impossible not to think about it constantly. The Observer has no choice but to give you what you constantly think about.

"I have been trying to open the door from my conscious mind to my subconscious mind to change some of the belief patterns I have. However, I have no idea what I am doing."

The journey in consciousness from the conscious mind to the subconscious mind is called the "Journey of the Master." It is precisely how we change our belief patterns. If you can place your attention on what it is that you want to become that represents what new belief you want to establish and you can give that concept all your attention for a period of time, your awareness will automatically move from the conscious mind to the subconscious mind. Once this process happens, you will have neurologically wired a new neuronet that will establish the new belief that leads to the new experience. This is my conclusion after having a conversation with JZ. This process is taught in detail in the Beginning Retreats. It would be to your great advantage to learn and practice this discipline at the school.

While this process is simple in theory, it is more difficult in its application. The three distractions that make this process difficult are the environment, the body, and time. In holding an image of your new belief in concentrated focus, there will be a battle with the environment and its distractions of noise, lights, and people, combined with the body and its difficulty in sitting quiet and motionless. When we add to that our constraints of time, which is everyone's scarcest commodity, we have the reasons why it is difficult to move consciousness to the subconscious mind through concentrated focus. It is, however, a skill that can be developed.

"Is there a shortcut to repetition? I seem to have to read information over and over to absorb it."

There is a shortcut to repetition, but the answer is harsh. The shortcut is to know that you do not need to read information over and over to absorb it and integrate it into your knowledge base. If you insist on knowing a shortcut, you will find the shortcut, just like Einstein did as he insisted on knowing about the mysteries of light. After ten years of insistence, his brain sent him the visions. He then had to learn the mathematics necessary to explain these visions. If you would learn how to Mind Map information, you would absorb it the first time you heard it and the information would be readily accessible for recall. Mind Mapping is a technique first introduced by Tony Buzan in the 1970s that uses pictures, colors, and key words to record information that is uniquely mapped in the brain for instant recall. You can Google Mind Mapping to get more information.

"A friend watched my eyes turn from brown to white about two years ago. I saw my eyes change one morning while looking in the mirror. While only two others have seen this change, it is starting to happen more often. Do you know what is happening?"

I do not know what is happening by your description but I do know that you can find out by posing this question to your own God. If you are sincere in wanting to know why it is happening and you are persistent with that intent, then the doors of opportunity to know will be open to you. Even a street person who smokes will always have cigarettes because it is their priority. No matter what else happens that day, they will arrange for enough money to buy their cigarettes. They have collapsed their intent into physical reality. You must want the answer with that same amount of persistence. You must become the Einstein of your own inquiry. Once you discover this connection to the mind of God, your days of needing to ask for anyone else's advice or understanding will be over.

"Why should I try to create my day if I am not feeling like an unlimited God and Spirit is getting in my way?"

Spirit is the life force that keeps us alive. Spirit is the essence of who you are and does not have an agenda. The soul has an agenda and it is expressed in the DNA encoded in every cell. The propensities of who we are as a genetic being are what get in our way. The personality is the characterization of these propensities and as such we are compelled to respond to our environment in certain and specific ways. When we sit down to create our day, if we have not prepared the brain properly the personality will override any conscious creation that is different from the life we are living. It sees the new hope or dream as a potential threat to our current lifestyle, and it is correct in its assumption.

We should only create our day when we are feeling unlimited, so it is important to get into the right frame of mind before that creative process. We do that in our school by preparing the brain with the C&E® breath technique. Once we have anesthetized the neocortex, we can present the new day to the brain without the brain's objection. So we are now feeling unlimited and we will be successful because we have prepared the brain properly before planting the seeds of our new realities.

"How long does it take to create a new neuronet to replace the one that has been hardwired for your entire life? What do you do if after doing your disciplines in the morning you find yourselves in your old neuronet during the day? How can you shift in a moment to get back on track?"

First of all, you do not replace one neuronet with another neuronet. You occupy a new one while leaving an old one. If you have the proper knowledge, the willingness to practice and a desire to change, a new neuronet can be occupied instantaneously.

The old neuronet needs attention to continue to be effective. If you can learn to observe those circumstances that activate the old neuronet without engaging it to the point of an emotional response, then it will die. The old attitude cannot survive as a neurological network if you do not respond to it. Observation is not engagement. That is how you get rid of an old attitude. When you do your disciplines in the morning, they are practiced in order for you to create that new neurological attitude. However, they must be reinforced throughout the day in order for them to become as hardwired as were the old attitudes. If you find yourself wanting to respond as the old attitude, then you must step back and simply observe the situation as if you were a disinterested party. If you can do this several times consistently, then you will have atrophied that connection and you will no longer be the person with the old attitude. That is how you get back on track.

"What does 'we take nothing personally' mean when we know that everything comes out of our own mind?"

If this is in the context of relationships, then it often means that what is being said to us by another is more of a reflection of that person than the comments that are being made. We do know that everything in our environment is a reflection of our own mind, and with this understanding we can be at peace without having to react emotionally to circumstances that might normally be difficult. In addition, we know that this constructed reality is an illusion in that it can be dreamed away and re-created. We don't take personally today what we can change tomorrow. So there are many ways to take responsibility for our creations without becoming involved emotionally. If we can reconcile our life in this manner, then we have reached a level of understanding that is precisely what we have been asked to do, to make known the unknown, our true spiritual journey.

"The sins of the father and the mother are visited upon their children."

Ramtha

Chapter 14

WISDOM

"I have read four of Ramtha's books, including *Ramtha: An Introduction, Change: the Days to Come, Soulmates, and A Beginner's Guide to Creating Reality*. I really like the ideas expounded and really, really agree with Ramtha but still find it hard to find anything that tells you what to do to get on the path back home, in other words, how to ascend from this lowest world and stop incarnating. My question is, is there anything you have read of his that really gives you a good guide to doing this? I know it is going to take a lot of time regardless, but those books just seem to point out wisdoms and not show how to ascend."

I knew from the first presentation I did in Auckland, New Zealand, in January 1999 that I had been properly and thoroughly prepared, having spent twenty-plus years in a School of Ancient Wisdom. One of the unique aspects of this school that sets it apart from almost all other organizations is that this school (RSE) teaches that knowledge in and of itself is only going to be philosophy. All philosophy in and of itself is void of experience. As Ramtha would say, "The graveyards are full of philosophers." When one has knowledge combined with experience, then we have personal truth, wisdom, and evolution. You must find a methodology that offers this sequence. Any true spiritual school or organization will provide this sequence so that dogma, superstition, and spiritual trash can be eliminated.

Ascension, the ultimate spiritual initiation, will require the sequence of scientific knowledge, ancient wisdom, and a discipline that leads to that experience. In 1982, at a small audience with Ramtha in San Francisco, I said that I had heard about ascension and that I would like to do it. Ramtha answered me by saying that my response sounded more like divine suicide. He went onto say that ascension was the result of a life well-lived and not something to which one aspired. A life well-lived had everything to do with "making known the unknown," the one and only law of God.

"Would you explain the relationship between change, karma, and the subconscious mind? Do we go beyond karma when we change?"

This is an excellent question. We must define karma with greater clarity than the definition used by the Hindus, which was defined as the reason we reincarnate. It is true that we reincarnate because of our karma, but we do not see karma as bad deeds from our past but rather as unfinished business. Everything we have not yet owned in the human drama will be brought forward in this genetic expression for the opportunity to own these emotions of limitation. So let's call karma our genetic propensity to behave in certain predictable ways.

We as human beings are greatly influenced by our genetic propensities. We are the product of the "sins of our mother and father," as it is insinuated in the Bible. This means that we have inherited their emotional limitations such as anger, fear, competition, unworthiness, and so on. In this life we will be driven to experience these same limited emotions in hopes that we will resolve our confusion and no longer express any or all of these in circumstances that once triggered these predictable emotions. Once we resolve or bring to wisdom an understanding with any of these genetic propensities, we have changed. This means that we have owned the karma of this propensity and it will no longer be passed on as a genetic expression. The moment we own all of our genetic propensities is the moment we have owned our humanity and we are without karma. We can conclude by answering this question that change eliminates karma, and once karma is eliminated we are under the leadership of our subconscious mind that is also called our holy, Holy Spirit or the mind of God.

When we don't resolve certain attitudes or continue to operate within certain emotional propensities, we reincarnate into a genetic body that gives us the greatest opportunity to face these same circumstances again. For instance, if a man does not resolve his emotions of jealousy, he will most likely be reborn into a culture that is highly emotional and one in which the man is constantly under the threat of a promiscuous wife or lover. This scenario gives him the greatest opportunity to realize that his jealously has nothing to do with his partner but rather his own insecurity and the fact that he is ignorant and does not know his eternal nature. This will continue lifetime after lifetime until there is understanding and resolution. This is how we pick genetic lines to be reborn into and how cultures are made up of souls that are all endeavoring to learn the same lessons. I have been privileged to see this throughout my travels around the world teaching large groups of students from specific cultures such as the Japanese, who are very different from the Italians, who are distinct and different from the Americans.

The problem of karma is that it is so undefined that most people handle karma by abstaining from life and hoping that they can move through this life without having offended or re-created the circumstances that add to the karmic bank account. So karma is not something to be afraid of or cautious around. It is the way, the path, and the life. Karma is our instructional manual for transformation, and we go about resolving each of those limited emotional responses to life in order to become transcendent of the human condition. All great beings are warriors in conquering their karma. Not one great being abstained from life to become a great being. All great beings are conquerors of their own limitations.

Every life you have is the greatest life you have ever had

because you are conquering each emotion that is still unresolved. Each life you may resolve only one genetic propensity but your next life will then be a concentration of those things yet to be brought to wisdom, and it continues to become a more and more concentrated life on those emotions left to be resolved. This often brings about the greatest adversity. Adversity defines a person and is often the only experience that will make enough of an impact to render change in a human being. A life of adversity is a life destined for great change. With knowledge, adversity is one of our greatest assets. Without knowledge, adversity is almost always seen as something being done to us and we become victimized by those circumstances.

People often take pride in who they think they have been in past lives. They claim to have been Nefertiti, one of the Caesars, a king, or Pharaoh. What is not understood by those making these claims is that this life, no matter how humble and uncelebrated, is the greatest evolved life so far. Even if only one emotion is owned as wisdom, you are greater than your last life and those previous to it.

The typical view of karma is that it is strictly a spiritual kind of bank account and nowhere else will you hear the information that it is actually manifesting in the DNA with which we are born.

"What I have lived before, is that imagination? I certainly cannot see or know at this moment what my past life was all about. So when people say that, where is that coming from?"

Conversations about past lives are interesting but rarely accurate for the following reason. The brain that we use in this life is new to this life and its experiences. The part of the brain we use ninety-nine percent of the time does not have past-life information stored in it. This new brain has the information from our genetics, education, and the experiences of this lifetime only. So when people casually recall their past lives, they do that in a romantic way. Do you know how many people think they were Cleopatra or some other famous and important person? And this past importance somehow justifies the mundane life that they are currently living.

Every person is living his or her most important life. What we have owned as wisdom is no longer a part of our genetic propensity that compels us to express certain emotions. Therefore the body we currently inhabit is giving us our greatest opportunity to continue to evolve. This lifetime is everyone's greatest lifetime even though we are probably not well-known or famous. We do not have to make up or hope that we have been something great in the past just because our current life does not emulate that same greatness. Most people do not realize that life is the gift and that this life in particular is the greatest opportunity we have had to become transcendent and to solve the mystery of being a human being.

To recall past lives, if that is important to you, can be done by accessing the part of your brain that holds that information. The lower cerebellum, the oldest part of the human brain, has this information stored and we call all of that information the mind of God. The mind of God contains the life experiences of the smallest microorganism to the greatest being that has ever lived, is living, or will live. The mind of God contains all of your past lives. If you can learn to access this part of the brain, which is one of the fundamental disciplines taught at RSE, you can know what you have been in your past.

"Can we also detach our dualistic thinking around karma as to whether it is good or bad?"

It is neither good nor bad. It is a job description. It is a list of those emotions that must be retired into wisdom. Your body is the perfect vehicle encoded genetically to ensure that you will have ample opportunity to confront these situations in life as they push the buttons of limited emotional responses. You will get these opportunities on a daily basis. The most difficult aspect of owning your emotions is that each and every one of these emotional responses will seem justified by the circumstances of your life.

Your feeling of abandonment will seem justified by the circumstances in your life, whether you created being given up for adoption by your biological parents or you were shunned by your father, or any number of circumstances that you could justify as the reason for you feeling abandoned. This example can be used with any other feelings of anger, sadness, envy, and jealousy, and the list goes on.

There are people who might think that this answer is not mystical enough. It might seem too easy. Who said that it had to be complicated? I think it is more accurate to say that those who do not like simple and accountable answers are looking for a way not to have to deal with taking responsibility for their own evolution. Those people would not like to be responsible for whether their list of emotional limitations gets shorter or remains the same. Change is not looked upon with favor by the personality. To the personality all change represents loss in one form or another. There are no spiritual sugar daddies who can shorten that list for you. You are the only one who can do that. A teacher can show us the way and create the doors of opportunity, but you and I must walk through those doors into the experience.

"Would you discuss the differences between the Holy Spirit, the Spirit, and God in relation to the soul as a perpetual recorder of experience?"

To simplify the above interaction, let us say that God is the Observer, always manifesting our thoughts with an unconditional love. Our Spirit is the traveler in space/time that is the essence housed in this body, and the soul is the secretary recording all of the experiences.

"What is the significance of children in our lives? How do children find their parents?"

Children are the greatest opportunity for parents to evolve.

Think about the interaction of the soul and its encoded DNA placed within the care of the two parents who pass along their DNA. The DNA being passed to the incoming child represents what the parents need to own as wisdom in their own lives. Now here comes an offspring with the exact characteristics of limitation that the parents have yet to own. What better opportunity for the parents on a day-to-day basis as they are confronted through the actions of their children to see the exact characteristics that they themselves need to own. This is the efficiency and the elegance of the soul. Every day we as conscious beings have the opportunity to resolve limited emotional reactions into resolutions of wisdom. If we can be the Observer of opportunities that once elicited emotional responses but now no longer do, we have owned some of the fractional aspects of our personality and have become more integrated, more whole, more evolved.

"If you were in a spacecraft traveling in a straight line at almost the speed of light and your windshield breaks, are you propelled faster than light at that moment, since the vacuum would suck you out?"

If you were in a craft of that level of advanced technology and the windshield broke, I would hope you would get sucked out for not having checked the specifications of forces upon it before you left on your trip.

"What is the spiritual training and the concept of breatharians who need no external food?"

I was in Belgium doing an Introductory Evening presentation for our school. After the talk, a lady came up to me and said, "I am a breatharian. I am very illuminated because of this practice and I am waiting for you to tell me why I should attend this Retreat." I simply looked at her and said, "If your discipline is so illuminating, why couldn't you answer that question for yourself?" She had no answer because she and so many others without knowledge think that if they do something extreme to their bodies that they are automatically on a spiritual path. People create all kinds of disguises to be considered special. When you cannot create intentional reality on your own terms, you can be seduced into creating an identity in which you appear special. That is someone wanting to be a guru.

So many people have the idea that being spiritual means only being pious, that you cannot be silly, laugh out loud, dance, or eat anything you want.

This is an old mind-set perpetrated by organizations that needed to keep their teachers, priests, rabbis, and ministers acting the way they wanted their constituents to act so that they could maintain control over them. Truly enlightened beings do not restrict themselves in any way because they live their lives beyond good and bad and right and wrong.

"Can you talk about insecurity? It seems to be rampant."

Insecurity is rampant because people do not know who they are. With a little knowledge it can become one of our greatest assets. Insecurity is beautiful because it gives us an opportunity to see what we have been using that has created a false security that is outside of ourselves. Secondly, we have an opportunity to clarify and understand what changes we must make to become secure within ourselves. If we can observe without judgment our own insecurity, it will vanish. The greatest temptation is to look for another source of support outside of ourselves. When we do this, we are only postponing the events that will lead to the same emotions of insecurity. The true spiritual journey is facing our fears, however they present themselves. With observation they will always become unmasked and powerless. Facing a fear is the only option for resolution, and with this act of courage we have owned another aspect of our fragmented personality that could only react emotionally to our environment. Every time we resolve an emotional reaction and we no longer have an emotional reaction to that same circumstance, we have changed the DNA in the nucleus of every cell. Therefore the signals being sent to each cell have changed and this means that the cells produce different proteins. This whole process is what restores the body to a greater level of health.

"When Ramtha has said that you are the path, what does that mean?"

It means that you are everything you need to overcome in order to evolve spiritually. The soul and its action are the greatest justice system ever devised. When Ramtha says that we are here to conquer ourselves, he is saying that we must individually master our habitual emotional responses to our environment. Simply said, what bothers you in your life, once mastered, will no longer bother you. In other words, you have owned the wisdom of those circumstances and are no longer compelled to respond in the same ways you did before. These are the responses of anger, fear, doubt, envy, lack, etc. We can all name the emotions by which humanity is controlled.

Each of us is wearing our own journey to enlightenment. In each incarnation the soul encodes our DNA with the exact genetic propensities necessary to ensure that we will react in the same emotional ways that we have in the past. Conquering ourselves will resolve each of these predictable responses into no response. Now you are on the true spiritual journey by resolving into wisdom each item on the soul's agenda. This process is what we are to do in fulfilling God's only law. However, the end result is not a person who is no longer emotional; it is a person who is free. The natural state of freedom is joy, which is the absence of predictable emotions.

The first step is to get rid of the unfinished business that is encoded as genetic propensities. Everyone will know what they are when they simply observe their own behaviors in a variety of experiences and note which emotions are always triggered with which circumstances. This is the design of the soul in action. It is designed to get us to react genetically (habitually) in hopes that we might tire of this behavior and make a new choice. We will eventually come to the understanding that emotions are the unfinished business of an opportunity and that wisdom lies on the other side of these emotions as understanding. We retire each genetic configuration in our DNA as we own each of these habitual responses. This ownership creates a whole cascade of changes. With each resolution the DNA is changed. The signal now sent from the template of the DNA to the cells is changed, and those cells produce different proteins as the new building blocks for cellular expression. Remember, youth and longevity are correlated to change, and this is the biology of that process.

You cannot get anywhere without resolving these emotions. You will simply be playing out a genetic program, and this is humanity's greatest distraction and secret. I call it a secret because our responses will always seem justified. They are genetically programmed and will feel right every time. Without knowledge, there is little chance for change. In addition to knowledge, there must be a methodology to utilize the knowledge so that change can be accomplished.

"What exactly would you do if you lived in another country in circumstances that are not great and tried to understand enlightenment, yet all around you evidence suggests that the world is like hell. What would you suggest is the best way to break through? I would dearly love an answer to that question but different from what most self-help books suggest. They don't work for the majority."

The first thing that one must do is to ask a question similar to the one you asked, which questioning begins the journey to enlightenment. Many years ago I posed a question similar to yours, that there must be something more to life than what I or anyone else I knew was experiencing. It is that question that leads to a door of opportunity. If you walk through the first door, then another door will appear, and this process continues until you succeed or stop going through the doors.

The world is never going to mirror back to you anything other than what you have programmed in your brain. That program is called mind. Your mind expands as you gather more knowledge and more experience. Your world will change accordingly. As Gandhi said, "Become the change you want the world to be." That is exactly how it works. When you change, you will no longer experience the oppression of the world and its continuous presentation of your former mind and its reflection back to you .

All cultures maintain their traditions through rules, regulations, and social mores by which their constituents must abide. The consequence of not obeying these traditions is to be ostracized, and these institutions know that human beings have an overwhelming need to belong and will rarely sacrifice this need to become an individual ideal.

Knowledge of who we are, where we come from, what our purpose is, and how we can fulfill that purpose allows us to transcend our cultures and begin the true spiritual journey. Once this journey becomes our singular intent, we will have transcended our culture and our world-view will have changed dramatically. No longer will it reflect a world that is like hell but rather a world of unlimited choices, possibilities, and opportunities.

What is remarkable about Ramtha's knowledge is that it is easily accessible. You don't have to go searching all over the world for the masters who have this understanding. Those masters who have this knowledge are not visible for the most part or might teach a small group of students. None have the accessibility of RSE. Ramtha has said that this is a rare school that is open to the common person. All you have to do to learn this knowledge is make it to the school and pay for the classes. It is not only rare but original and unique. I have made presentations to thousands of students over the past eight years and not one person has compared the school to some other organization or discipline. That tells me that it is radically different from anything else being offered for personal transformation.

"In addition to its uniqueness, when you observe students in other cultures is it true that all cultures respond

in a similar way?"

Being self-empowered in any culture is received with great enthusiasm. Statistics of eighty-four to ninety percent of those who attend the Beginning Retreat reporting that it is "the greatest week of their life, so far," are cross-cultural. The results of those questionnaires are consistent in all six continents that the training is held.

"I am frustrated in not being able to see the lines while making the sign of the triad, a sacred symbol that communicates to our subconscious mind that we are preparing our body to do the miraculous."

The most important aspect of any discipline is the sincerity in which you approach the discipline, and that is as important as the technique itself. The God within has tremendous leeway for students who are perfecting the technique and it is always the intent that is manifested. Sincerity, which represents being in the moment with clear intent, will always bear fruit regardless of the perfection of the technique. The techniques are utilized as a focal point until they are no longer needed. However, even the most advanced students in the school still use the techniques as they were originally taught. Making the sign of the triad lets the subconscious mind know that you know some things about yourself: You know where you have come from, you know who you are, you know what your destiny is, and you know how to fulfill that destiny. This sign is the symbol that contains all that knowledge and facilitates the student who has been initiated into that knowledge to begin preparing the brain for creation.

"I have average psychic ability and I have premonitions of death, major illnesses, and milestone events with certain people. I am afraid by getting a premonition of someone that I may actually be contributing to the manifestation of that person. Is that possible since I have seen a number of these events in my life? I am finding this a bit distressing.

Is there a way to change this person's future, knowing what I have already seen?"

Why would anyone want to change another person's future? They would have to be assessing it from their own point of view rather than the point of creation from the other person. We all have opinions of how we think other people's lives should evolve. It is human nature to want to help someone who seems to have had a catastrophic event or major illness and alleviate that experience. However, I have seen many people, including myself, who would not change those catastrophic events, at least in retrospect, for they became the experiences that were life-changing. These are experiences that we would not have had the courage to consciously create for ourselves. It is our God that has that ultimate compassion to see us through those times and events.

Premonitions that are perceived as events with others would be better viewed in a more personal context. The reason for this is simple. Every person, place, thing, time, and event in our lives is frequency specific to us. We are the creators of our own experience and nothing is reflected in our world that is not an aspect of ourselves. Each of us is the director, producer, and writer of our own play. Each actor in our play is well-rehearsed and following our script. What is interesting is that our actors have their own plays running in theaters next to ours in which we may be one of their well-rehearsed actors. Shakespeare, an initiate in a secret society, said it well. "Life is but a stage, full of sound and fury, signifying nothing." This was a precursor to the Many-Worlds Theory. Now we can adjust our concept and concern that we are so powerful that we are having a direct and profound effect on another person. We are having a profound effect on ourselves and it will be reflected in our environment in the people, places, things, times, and events in our lives. In other words, there is one person in the audience even though it looks like a full house. We all live in a self-enclosed, precisely designed theater being entertained by the characters of our mind. The implications of this are vast. With this understanding you can truly take responsibility for everything that happens in your life, and you have the secret that allows you to rewrite the script for any one person in your play. It is the ultimate self-empowering theory that is popularly called the many-worlds in physics.

The beauty of this understanding is that you can more easily own your limited emotional reactions to the people in your life because you understand that they are placed there to help you accept everything about yourself. When what bothered you before about them bothers you no more, you are in the momentum of evolution as it is designed to be.

"Is there an individual soul, maybe not separate from everyone else, but nonetheless individual? For me, individual self must persist. For instance, Christ achieved the ultimate level of consciousness but not you and not me."

Absolutely, we are all individuals with individual souls. The soul was created to record the experiences of each individual. The concept of a collective soul is not very exciting. Imagine the idea that when you become enlightened it would be analogous to a water molecule becoming a part of the whole ocean. This is a much too homogenized concept to excite a creator. There is individuality as far into time as one can imagine. However, your idea of Christ achieving the ultimate level of consciousness is not accurate. He may have achieved a greater level of mind than you and I, so far, but he is still on a journey of discovery. How can someone stop creating? Even that is a creation. So there is no end to learning for anyone, including our idea of the most advanced being.

We never lose our individuality on the spiritual path. Most individual identities become lost to the world and its promotional idea of what a person should be like to be successful. In most cases people have no individual identity when they begin a spiritual journey. Most people have been successfully indoctrinated by their culture. Culture is reinforced to maintain boundaries of behavior, not individuality. If you are a part of the world and its values, then you are not an individual, even though the soul is the mechanism that assures your individuality into eternity.

"What does owning mean?"

In its simplest understanding through personal experience, "What bothered you before bothers you no more." For example, you are always upset that your husband puts the bowls away in the wrong cupboard and you cannot understand what is so difficult about the procedure. You are continuously agitated by the same action until one day you simply remove the bowl from the wrong cupboard and put it in its rightful place. If it is done in a complete matter-of-fact way without emotion or judgment, you have owned a predictable habit that is no longer on an automatic response. You have now evolved your response, which is mastering yourself.

If we can learn to observe ourselves and know that we create all circumstances, it becomes easier to own our habitual responses. With practice it does become easier. The two problems we have are that we forget who is creating the whole circumstance because it seems so real and, secondly, we do not readily give up addictions. One of the problems we face additionally is that people want their emotions because it defines them as an individual and they think that without those responses that life would be dull and predictable. It is already dull and predictable with the same expressed emotions. It isn't that you are to become devoid of emotions but that you will experience new emotions based on new thoughts. Just like the children of the Bronx, if you cannot predict the outcome of a new experience, you will not venture in that direction. This is the reluctance of the majority of humanity.

"Do we have to be careful about tapping into infrared entities?"

Infrared entities have great information. They live in an extraordinary environment. To learn about someone does not mean we have to act the way they act. Are there weird entities in the infrared plane? Yes, because they have not gone on into full progression. They are hanging around the Earth plane because they are addicted to their past and the habits of that life, so they are going to be a little strange to us. They often appear to us as shadows and apparitions. It is superstition and fear that has kept most people from understanding the true spiritual journey and its steps of evolution.

"In the *Creating Personal Reality* video, what is the meaning of the hand gesture Ramtha uses when he says, "So be it"? Some of the students seem to be crying during the C&E® breath discipline. Why do they do that? And, lastly, in the Great Hall I saw a six-sided star at one end of the hall. What is its significance?"

The hand gesture is an ancient sign that means, "This that I am about to do is already manifested," and the master says, "So be it!" When something is undertaken with a mind that knows it already is, then the reality must follow that direction. It is done in absolute certainty.

The tears are associated with freedom, not sadness. When students finally get free of the restrictions of their limited minds, the experience of freedom is often accompanied with tears. In the C&E® process, this happens to some students when their energy moves out of the first three seals and moves up into the fourth seal. It is not something that continues. Once you reach this level of mind on a more consistent basis, the tears are replaced with the familiarity of that experience. I have had the privilege of observing this in the Beginning Retreats, for I am one of the appointed teachers who teaches this discipline. In talking to the students who are surprised by this reaction, they always report that the tears are not associated with anything sad but a spontaneous reaction to the experience of freedom.

At both ends of the Great Hall, there are symbols. The six-sided star is called the Initiate Star. It is two intersecting triangles. The one on top is blue and the one on the bottom is red. It represents having owned the lower seals associated with sexuality, pain, and power. These are the characteristics of the attitudes of humanity. The blue triangle represents a master's journey in making known the unknown. This symbol is also called the Star of David and was inscribed into Solomon's ring, which signified unparalleled wisdom.

"Can you tell me why we have been created this way to experience life in such a difficult way? I have been trying to get in touch with the Source. Maybe there are beings that are consuming our lower emotions just like we consume animals."

The reason why it is difficult here is because this is the plane of demonstration. Whatever we have yet to own is going to be the genetic propensities that throw us into those situations again. It is designed for ownership, not difficulty. Without the knowledge that this is the design, we continue to react with our limited emotions to circumstances that do not automatically require those reactions. For example, we always get confused when someone begins to talk about science, or we become jealous or afraid when our spouse talks about wanting more space, or anything else to which we might react. So it appears that this incarnation is stacked against us. It is an opportunity to evolve. If you can understand this, then you want the adversities of life so that you can own the experiences without reaction. This is the true spiritual journey and the only path of evolution.

We are in the slowest level of reality. As such, our dreams unfold in a slow and timely manner. This can be very frustrating to an entity who can remember thinking a thought and it manifesting in the next moment. However, the safeguard is that we have thoughts that we would rather not manifest in the next moment of reality, and we can rethink them before they slowly manifest. Until we mature, this level of reality has its benefits. However, many people lose hope in their dreams because they do take so long to become realized. If you hold onto a dream with the attitude that you will do whatever it takes to create that reality, it will manifest in short order. Why? Because the Observer knows no time, and the attitude of whatever it takes indicates an absolute fortitude. This translates into a Now reality and manifests very quickly. Saying whatever it takes and meaning it is an absolute and always transcends time.

"In twenty-five words or less, how do you kill doubt?"

You don't kill it. To try to kill something only empowers it. You observe it without emotion and it will dissipate over time.

"Has Ramtha ever spoken about the book, *A Course in Miracles*? Has he recently spoken about the "Days to Come" and the coming Earth changes?"

When I first started going to the Ramtha teachings, the *Course in Miracles* was very popular and had been since the late seventies. I remember someone asking him about the book and his response was very short. He said they were tedious and boring. I laughed when he said that because I had found them that way but thought that maybe I didn't have the discipline or patience to understand them at their highest level. As a warrior, he would prefer to conquer something, himself mostly, rather than read and contemplate a sentence for a week. It is not in his nature to be that way. Now JZ has recently commented on the same book. She said that the beauty of that book was that it asked people to contemplate something lofty for a long enough period of time and that it stopped people from thinking in their normal way. If done properly, the book could help people to a greater understanding of themselves. I am sure they have been valuable for many people. But, remember, the school and Ramtha's teachings are based on a direct experience of the philosophy and not the philosophy alone.

The "Days to Come" were communicated to the public in 1986. Ramtha has told us for many years that the reason he started telling us back then was because humans are so slow to change. If you look at the state of the Earth, its pollution and global warming, the economic instability in world currencies, and the religious fervor that continues to separate and create violence, we are in the midst of those prophesied days. The bad news is that it can only get worse before it gets better. He recently said in a New York audience that the polar ice sheets would be melted in twelve years. That was an outrageous statement. However, the next day *Time* magazine reported that global warming was reaching its critical mass with irreversible and catastrophic effects in the very near future.

The students in our school have been preparing for such reactions for many years and have fortified their resources to such a degree that they are relatively immune to economic collapse, religious wars, or geophysical changes. You should take the same precautions. There are wonderful books that outline the necessary resources for sustaining a family over a certain period of time. Even the U.S. Department of Homeland Security is recommending that families stockpile a two-week supply of food and water.

"Someone I have always enjoyed now seems to be projecting visions of destruction. What causes seemingly enlightened teachers to lean toward negative ideas?"

First we have to understand that we carry our own bias of destruction as being negative. There is an old Chinese story of the son of the wise man who broke his ankle one day. Most of the townspeople came to the wise man to give their condolences. However, the wise man said that he did not see the accident as negative or positive. As it turns out, the province became engaged in a vicious battle and his son was left at home to heal. While many of the young men were killed in this battle, the son of the wise man was spared. When we do not place a judgment on a circumstance, it has the freedom to unfold in an unpredictable and surreptitious way.

If we do not automatically see destruction as a negative concept, it has the opportunity to transmute into a higher form of organization, like the phoenix that rises from the ashes in a rebirth. If we can develop the skill of observation rather than jumping to a judgment that includes a polarized response, we can begin to think like the Chinese wise man or a master who has seen the virtue of not concluding an experience. Once we judge an experience, then the quantum field must unfold that reality in personal terms that satisfy the judgment. Observation allows for the grace of an unpredictable and unexpected manifestation. It is the way masters think and observe life.

Positive and negative originated with the particles that belong to the environment of visible light. Both particles are necessary to create this three-dimensional reality. Men are constructed of a positive energy and women in their receivership are a negative energy. It requires the two polarized energies to create a new life, concept, or manifestation. It is the judgment that positive is good and negative is bad that reinforces a personality of prejudice. Judgment will always produce an emotion, while observation is without emotion, and most people are unwilling to live life without the chemistry of repetitive emotions.

"What is your explanation about Down syndrome? What unresolved emotional issues would the parents have to create such an offspring?"

The parents might have emotional issues that make it difficult to deal with such an unusual child. It might be impatience, as these children are easily frustrated. It might be embarrassment, fear, or any other reaction that is the result of taking care of these unique children. Imagine how evolved one would become as they learned to unconditionally love these children. That would mean that they have unconditionally loved themselves. These children are a rare gift to their parents, and they often make these arrangements before incarnation in an ultimate act of love. Ramtha has told us that some of the children who have been diagnosed as multiple personalities have returned to demonstrate that different parts in your brain have different effects on your body. If you can learn to move in your brain, you can learn to heal your life.

The opportunity parents have with their children is that everything they have yet to own is packaged as a primary reflection in their children. You get to have dinner with this reflection every night. Ramtha told me that if I could learn to love my oldest son, then I would have learned to love everyone else in the process. In raising my oldest son, he represented everything that still bothered me. To love him was my opportunity to own everything yet unowned in myself. He has afforded me that gift, and I took advantage of it by learning to love him unconditionally. You can only love in another what it is you have come to love in yourself. This is the greatest gift our children give us.

"What has Ramtha said about the Wingmakers?"

He told us that they represented a potential future. He has not mentioned them for over a decade.

"Since we all came from Point Zero with the same divinity within, why did some of us come in the form of apes with our first incarnation on Earth? I thought there were Gods here already, and didn't they give us an evolutionary boost with their spliced DNA?"

We are destined to return to an environment with the specific DNA that would allow us the greatest opportunity to evolve by making known the unknown. Four hundred and fifty-five thousand years ago the Earth provided the greatest opportunity for some of us to incarnate. It was a splendid choice in that we as primitive entities were crossbred with a superior race and instantly upgraded to a much more intelligent species. This gap in anthropological terms represents the "missing link" that has been discussed in universities for decades. Cro-Magnon evolved from Neanderthal one million years more quickly than would have been predicted by anthropologists. This has been one of the unsolved mysteries in scientific academia. So much new information is coming to the surface. Archeologists have recently uncovered a flute that has been carbon-dated to 35,000 years ago. The new archeologists who are committed to truth will continue to reveal artifacts that will be one of the springboards to a new paradigm of historical understanding.

"Space and time are not modes in which we live, but modes in which we think."

Albert Einstein

Chapter 15

First Meeting

"What is the most significant moment you have experienced with Ramtha?"

It was the first time I met Ramtha at a two-day weekend workshop in Federal Way, a suburb of Seattle. I had heard a cassette tape of a Dialogue (what these weekends were called) and instantly I wanted to see the entity who was the mind behind what I had heard on that tape. I called the organization and they told me that the next opportunity was one month later near Seattle. I signed up and waited for my opportunity.

On March 19, 1982, on our flight from San Diego to Seattle, the captain came on the intercom and announced that we had just passed over the top of Mt. St. Helens and that it had just exploded with its second historic blast. I looked at the person traveling with me and said, "This is going to be a very big weekend."

The next day, March 20, I was waiting for Ramtha in a room in Federal Way. He made an appearance and all of a sudden the room went completely white. The only thing I could see were his two eyes, nothing else. A bomb could have gone off and I would not have noticed. That first day included Ramtha addressing certain individuals in the room and working with each of them to discover what they wanted. Once he established what they wanted, he simply said, "So be it." At the end of the day he did what was called the "Christ Raising." I do not think that was ever done again.

There were about forty people standing in a circle. Ramtha stood in front of each person and while touching his own seals one by one, he touched the corresponding seal of the participant. In watching this process it did not appear to be of any real significance in the moment. When he stood in front of me and began the process, I was once again transfixed by his eyes and completely absorbed in the moment. When he finished with me and moved to the next person I thought I was going to pass out. I was feeling faint and could barely stand up. I was toward the end of the line and remained standing through pure will, not wanting to fall down and make a scene.

As soon as he left the room I went to the rental car outside and sat in the driver's seat and literally shook for twenty minutes. When it was over I went to dinner with my friend and drank several glasses of wine to reestablish a relationship with my former self. That was the first day I met Ramtha and I have not been the same since.

I have had the privilege, and still do, to interact with him. I have been a staff member of this organization for eighteen years, an administrator of the events for twelve years, and a teacher for the past nine years. These positions give me the opportunity to speak with him on occasion. In the beginning of his teachings Ramtha performed a lot of miracles, granting to some whatever it was they asked for. I was witness to some of these. Some people called him "Ramtha Claus" because he was famous in manifesting what people asked.

I told all of my friends about this great Master Teacher, that he was the genie who granted wishes. All of them came to see him and asked him to manifest for them their dreams. He said, "So be it" to all of them. And now twenty-four years later not one of them is current in his school. Not even once in all of those sessions did someone ask Ramtha if he would teach them how to manifest their own dreams. No one even asked Ramtha how he did it. We just wanted our wishes granted. Therefore after a few years the Dialogues were discontinued and the sessions with Ramtha, called Intensives, became one-, two-, and three-day specialty teachings.

I have seen the transition from Dialogues to Intensives and from the Intensives to the school, established in 1988. The school was finally established to teach a group of sincere students how to manifest their own created reality.

"You are the only Observer
in your environment."

Ramtha

Chapter 16

HIGH HOLIDAYS

"Do you have any thoughts about the Christmas season?"

It is one of the only times that we break from our habit of consumerism and think of other people. It is considered the high holidays because we do something different for a few weeks, and remarkably it is the most joyous time of the year. I lived in New York for several years and it was the only time of the year that New Yorkers smiled on a consistent basis, and they even smiled at strangers during the holidays. Anyone from New York knows that this is unusual behavior at any other time of the year.

Giving without conditions is the basis for joy and satisfaction. Giving is the secret to fabulous wealth. The beauty of this is that only those who are truly abundant give unconditionally. No one in lack ever thinks about giving, because the act itself is counterintuitive. Wealth has its own built-in safety device. To become wealthy is an attitude. My favorite saying regarding wealth is a Chinese proverb, "A rich man is one who has enough." We all know that when we have enough we are more apt to share what we have with others. Christmas is the season we give without resenting that we are giving up something, and joy is abundant during this time.

The high holidays are the time for giving, and the winter season in general is a time for contemplation. I love the winter.

It is the greatest time to reflect on what you have accomplished during the previous year, i.e., did you realize your dreams from the previous winter? Ramtha, a lover of nature, his only true teacher, has made us aware that all of nature dreams during the winter and that in the spring those dreams begin to unfold in the form of new shoots, leaves, flowers, and buds of fruit. We have been taught to do the same as nature.

Winter is a time of long nights and shorter days, perfect for being inside and contemplating new realities. At the end of the high holidays, the end of the year, and after contemplating our accomplishments and the things that have yet to manifest, we create the reality of our coming new year. When this is done properly and we go through the entire new year as if we were reviewing it during the high holidays of the next year, we are properly creating reality. Like all of nature, our buds of reality begin to unfold in the spring and continue throughout the year to be reviewed once again at the end of the high holidays. When we do this we are in alignment with nature and the forces of nature are in harmony with our own creations.

We can use the example of the caterpillar and the butterfly, a true metamorphosis. The caterpillar, a short, fat, stubby-legged creature, finishes eating its leaves of summer and intuitively finds a broad leaf to crawl under to spin its cocoon. In this darkened environment of privacy, it has the proper home in which to dream its dream of flight. After twenty-eight days it emerges as a creature of exquisite beauty. Instead of green leaves, it feasts from the nectar of deep-throated flowers. This is how Ramtha describes the process of metamorphosis that he takes his students through.

We don't have to get caught up in the commercialism. There is a lot more to this season than what we see on TV. I had an amazing experience at our school several years ago at the annual Christmas party for the children. My son was four and a half years old and he was sitting by the section that displayed the gifts for the four- to six-year-olds. There is a large thirty-foot tree in the middle of the hall in our school that is surrounded by gifts for all the children divided into age groups up to thirteen years old. My son and another boy were sitting across from a gift that both of them wanted. They wouldn't run around and play with the other kids for fear of losing their position next to the gift they both wanted. I was watching with considerable interest to see what was going to happen when they were allowed to get the gift they wanted. A few minutes before the four- to six-year-olds were to choose and get their gift, my son asked the boy if he really wanted the gift they both had their eye on. "Yes," was the immediate answer. My son hugged the little boy and told him that he would take the Lego castle and leave the other more preferred gift for him.

My son got the Lego castle, which was very large. I had already broken it down, put it into three plastic bags, and taken it to our car to be driven home later. There were a few gifts left over and some of the children who had not come to the evening were having the gifts put away for them. One of the staff came up to me and said, "By the way, one of those presents that your son wanted is still under the tree." We looked, and to our surprise no one else had taken it nor had we even seen it. My son said, "Dad, go get the Lego castle so that we can exchange it for this gift."

There are some events in the course of a normal day that are bigger than life. There are few things that can compare with a justice system this profound. Remember, giving is the secret to wealth and this story exemplifies this concept beautifully. How is it that nobody wanted this gift or that it escaped the eye of my son? The real question is, "Was the gift always there or did it show up to fulfill an abundant destiny, always the result of giving?"

"A garden is half-made
when it is well planned.
The best gardener is the one
who does the most gardening
by the winter fire."

Liberty Hyde Bailey
Botanist

Chapter 17

Affirmations

"Would you please explain the difference between the following three ways to affect the subconscious mind: using positive affirmations, focusing on an image, and subliminals? For example, the *Beginning C&E®* videotape contains subliminals but most people don't know it, so how come they have an effect on us when we are not even aware of them?"

First of all, the Beginning C&E® videotape does not contain subliminals. I was one of three people who edited and produced that product, and there are no subliminals at all.

The reason subliminals are effective is because the subliminal information is designed to bypass the conscious centers in the brain that automatically object to change. If you can be listening to information without objection, it stands a much greater chance of being accepted and then created as a reality.

Affirmations are the least effective means of reaching the subconscious mind, where all new creations take place, because they go against the existing reality. For instance, you are saying "I am fabulously wealthy," but if everything in your environment goes against that affirmation you are going to have a difficult time convincing yourself that wealth is your reality. The second reason affirmations are a poor manifesting technique is because they are generally used to override an existing condition such as lack of financial resources, illness, insecurity, doubt, and the list goes on. When a person is affirming a statement that is to override an existing condition, they are actually empowering the very condition they are trying to overcome, and that is the way the brain would register that attempt at change.

Affirmations only work when they are accompanied with a state of mind that has no judgment on the new potential reality. We must move consciousness out of the part of the brain that enjoys the current reality. Every situation in your life has benefits to the existing programs in your brain. Any new suggestion will have to be assessed and weighed by those same programs. In order to get a fair trial you have to present this potential to an impartial jury, and that is not possible unless you move your awareness to the part of the brain that has no judgment (midbrain).

If you use your brain properly and focus on an image that represents what you want to create, you have the most powerful tool for manifesting a new reality. You must be able to move your consciousness (awareness) to the part of the brain that is out of linear time (midbrain). When you reach a state of trance, you are beyond the part of the brain that would object to this new reality. A trancelike state has a similar effect to nitrous oxide in a dentist's office; your concerns are minimized. If this is done properly, you will have created a neurological acceptance in the brain (neuronet), and that reality will be on your timeline. You need a system for feedback to know when you are using your brain properly and that is what is taught at RSE.

An activity that most closely resembles this trancelike state is when you are driving down the highway and finally realize that you have not been aware of driving for the past several minutes, you have missed seeing the road signs, you have missed recognizing some of the exists, and you cannot remember what you had been thinking about. This state is called analogical mind and it simply means that you are one hundred percent focused on what you are thinking and nothing else in the environment has your attention.

Analogical mind is the secret to creating reality. When you

learn how to consciously create this state of mind, you have the secret to the kingdom of heaven. The greatest disciplines taught at RSE are how to move into a state of analogical mind.

"Can you expand on the concept of the trance? People might want to say, well, this is artificial, I am creating an artificial situation, and maybe this is hypnosis."

Trance means that you are disconnecting from the automatic programs of response. You have moved out of the neocortex and into the midbrain. This is the beginning of the Journey of the Master that is creating a new reality. If we never leave the neocortex, then we are subject to the realities of its existing programs. It is in the midbrain that we continue to focus on this new potential. If we stay focused without interruption, this concept will move into the lower cerebellum and follow the laws of quantum physics.

Quantum physics says that each of us is an Observer, that we are observing upon a field of infinite potentials, and that we collapse the reality this is consistent with our thoughts and our beliefs. If this new concept is presented to this part of the brain, then that is the concept that is collapsed into one's life experience.

These neurological programs are so powerful that they can override circumstances in life that would normally have a life-changing effect. While I was in college in the mid sixties, the counterculture was in full swing. One of my friends was from a wealthy family in New York and his father was a successful attorney. While in college, my friend indulged in some of the stronger drugs and became drug-addicted. When I saw him years later in Los Angeles, he was a financial consultant and later became an attorney. His ability to overcome an addiction and become a successful attorney had everything to do with those genetic programs that existed in his brain.

It isn't that we create artificial situations; it's that all situations are artificial. All realities are illusionary if they can be dreamed away and, as you can see, all realities can be dreamed away.

"Then going back to this idea of affirmations and saying I am not going to think negatively, I am going to think positively, are those moments practically worthless?"

They are not worthless. They actually continue to reinforce the programs you are trying to overcome, so they become an asset to the old programs (personality).

If you are saying affirmations to heal the body, they rarely work, for several reasons. You cannot heal the body with the same level of mind that created the affliction in the body. You must occupy a level of mind that has dominion over the physical body. Without knowing how to do this, how are you going to accomplish that feat? The body is affected by frequency. All frequency carries information according to the level of mind that is sending the thought. All disease in the body is a result of thoughts and the emotions associated with those thoughts. An affirmation that says "I am radiant health" is being said to overcome the current condition of nonradiant health. So nonradiant health is the greater reality in your mind and thus gets empowered. Unless you can achieve a state of mind that is greater than the thoughts that led to the disease, you will not heal the body through consciousness.

When you can reach a level of mind that is nonpolarized, you can heal with the energy of a unified field. Up to that point you will only reinforce the affliction. We don't use affirmations in our school without reaching a level of mind that allows these affirmative statements to become effective.

Affirmations can work if you do them long enough because you are going to go into a trance state, and this state is produced by the part of the brain that will accept the new concepts without objection. I was a long-distance runner for over ten years. I ran between two and twelve miles most days. At about forty-five minutes into my run, on those days that I ran the longer distances, I noticed that I developed that familiar trance state. I would then begin my affirmations for the remainder of the run. I had fabulous results doing affirmations in this manner. What made the process effective was introducing the concepts after my awareness had moved to the midbrain where these affirmations could be accepted without consideration. If I had introduced these affirmations without reaching this state of awareness, each affirmation would be weighed against the current reality and easily dismissed as fantasy. Affirmations work if the brain is properly prepared, similar to planting a seed in enhanced soil with the proper nutrient and moisture balance. The soil must be properly prepared to produce the fruit.

This was the methodology I used to create reality before I understood the mechanics of the brain. Looking back I see how I used affirmations in their most effective way by preparing the brain before introducing the concepts. I affirmed my fabulous wealth and my radiant health and I became fabulously wealthy and enjoyed radiant health to the extent that I was never sick one day during those ten years. Knowledge is the key to opportunity. Once you have the knowledge you need the techniques required to apply that knowledge in a precise way to create the desired results in your own life. This is the genius of Ramtha's School of Enlightenment.

"I have recently been reading a book that contains a meditation at the end of each chapter to help you relax and dwell on a few affirmations. The author suggests that you slow down your breathing before you begin to say the statements. Would it be valuable if I recorded on tape any affirmations I am going to say and then prepare myself for five minutes before the recording begins?"

I have always said that affirmations repeated without moving to the part of the brain that accepts new concepts creates the opposite intent, so it would be beneficial to prepare the brain in order to accept these new concepts. Recording the affirmations and listening to them with a background of meditative music would help you to go into a deeper level of mind. Moving into the deeper levels of mind is moving into the area of the brain that will accept the new concepts without objection. The acid test is whether these new concepts manifest into your life.

They will if you can repeat them or actively listen to them in a trancelike state. A light trance means that you have moved out of the area of the brain that always objects to new ideas.

Another advantage to listening to affirmations that are created by someone else is that they are not your affirmations. When we create affirmations, they are always about what we are trying not to be. For example, if an affirmation is stated that "I always have the time necessary to complete all my work," then the person obviously does not have the time necessary to complete their work and this is what gets reinforced into one's life. So when we create our own affirmations, if we do not prepare the brain properly we almost always create the opposite effect of the affirmation itself.

"If any organism fails to fulfill its potentialities,
it becomes sick."

William James
American Psychologist

Chapter 18

FREQUENCY

"Will you explain the bands?"

The bands are electromagnetic fields of energy that surround the body. It can be best described as looking like a teardrop that encompasses the physical body and shimmers like a soap bubble. There are two bands of electromagnetic energy that surround the body. There is a specific reason for two bands rather than the popular New Age notion of an aura, a band of energy surrounding the head.

"If the bands are creating the pattern of the body and holding it in place, why then when a person dies and the soul leaves permanently doesn't the body simply disintegrate? We have seen that on Star Trek. Some aliens do that when they die. Their whole physical body completely vanishes."

The body lives in a different time and a different frequency than the soul and Spirit. When the soul and Spirit pull away from the body, all the cells implode in the body. The cells, the components of the body, are no longer being held together by your Holy Spirit. Vanishing would happen if the body's frequency instantly increased upon death beyond the Hertzian frequency. The rule of thumb is that the body that lives in time will decompose in that same time.

"Can you describe the infrared realm?"

It is the level of frequency just above the Hertzian environment. We live in our three-dimensional reality in the Hertzian frequency. When people die they go to the infrared realm in that transition. If these people have enough knowledge, they move into the tunnel toward the light and then proceed to a light review. However, without knowledge, with a strong urge to remain as a human, or those who have "died in Christ," people will stay in the infrared realm. They do not have the knowledge that would allow them to continue their journey.

Remember what Ramtha said when he was in Spain? He explained that the entities taught by the church were afraid to move on because of the potential of an eternity in hell and they would not budge from this realm. Ramtha's book, *The Plane of Bliss*, describes this journey in great detail. Some of the entities in this realm are called "dead in Christ." After they died, they continued to stay in suspended animation waiting for the return of Christ in order to awaken. Ramtha has told us that they are the most difficult to awaken. And even when the masters take on the look of Christ, these Christians were told to be aware of the Antichrist, and they stay deep in sleep and will not easily awaken until Christ returns. This is another tragic account of the effect of the church on its innocent followers.

"Any recommendations on how to master the out-of-body experience? Are there places we can go that we are not limited by our personality?"

All manifestations follow the same rules. What changes is the dream we are manifesting. The out-of-body experience does not occur outside of the body. It is the experience of moving into another dimension within the body. How we accomplish this is with knowledge and a desire for that experience. We have six other bodies enfolded in the soul that are located in the center of the chest. The heart is moved to the side to make room for a cavity that contains an etheric energy that weighs thirteen ounces, according to Ramtha. This cavity is the home of the soul and those six other bodies that are encased within it. We do not leave the body. We go within and move our awareness to one of those other bodies.

The desire to have this experience is enough to enact the process. If you continue to have this desire, you will have the experience when you least expect it. In the beginning you will find yourself in familiar surroundings. As long as you do not look at your body and identify with it, you will be able to move on. If you do identify with your body, you will find yourself immediately back in it. This is a great clue, that whatever or wherever you think in that dimension of faster time you will immediately find yourself. The beauty of this is that you can think about a friend and go there immediately. The distance has no bearing on the time it takes to get there.

To go where your personality is not limited means that you need information of locations that you would love to visit but that are not familiar to your personality. Once you are in that faster dimension, whether it is infrared or the light, you can think of a location and you will instantly go there. For instance, if you had a desire to go to the Rose Nebula, the City of Light, or Zeta Reticuli, you will find yourself there the instant you think of it.

"Can you explain the flashes of light that I have been seeing in my room for over a month? I would not have believed it except my daughter also saw them."

There are many possible explanations. Here are two of the most plausible. Lights can be an indication of another dimension of reality. If you read Ramtha's teaching on *Who Are We Really* in a series of books called the Fireside Series, you will get a definitive description of the entities that exist outside of this dimension. As soon as the students in our school became aware of dimensional entities and dimensional realities, we could see the lights of that reality on a consistent basis. So you are either seeing the entities of another dimension or the dimensions of another reality itself. In either case, your brain is beginning to see what your eyes have always seen. Children have always seen these lights. It is only after we have been educated that it becomes more difficult to see these other dimensions. When you see a cat appear to be watching something as it traverses across the room, it has a vision that allows it to see infrared energy. They have developed this asset for survival. We have de-evolved ourselves out of these special characteristics because we use technology as a replacement. However, children and animals have not been educated out of the ability to see higher dimensions.

"I would like to know what happens to the water when we are making a toast."

Ramtha has been toasting us since the beginning of his teachings in 1979 and he has taught us to toast ourselves by changing the frequency of the water through words and prayer. Water is in the form of a crystalline structure and can be programmed. When we hold our water before we drink it and make a prayer, blessing, or declaration, we are programming the water to hold that intent in its structure. If we infuse the water with a blessing and then drink it, we are drinking that very declaration and the water will have that effect on our body. There has been a great deal of research done on the molecular structure of water and how it can be changed through thought or blessings. Words carry a frequency, and the frequency of the words or the blessing impregnates the water. Then we drink the elixir that carries out the function of the blessing. It is a way to nourish ourselves through the elegance of our own mind. It is an ancient ritual but its understanding has been lost through time, suppression, and ignorance.

"In Ramtha's books, he often stresses the need to believe with passion in what you want in order to manifest it. In his teaching, *Soul 101*, part 3, he stresses the need to

repeat by rote and keep it in our mind throughout the day until it becomes second nature. These statements seem to be conflicting. Can you clarify?"

Both statements are true and both work equally well. When you become passionate about something you want, you have moved to the part of the brain that is frequency specific with that concept. The reason you are passionate is because that part of the brain being expressed as a neuronet is sending a new signal to the cells of the body to prepare it for the experience. Passion means that you are in the part of the brain that can manifest that exact reality. You must become passionate in order to know that you have moved to the part of the brain that can manifest it. That is one way we accomplish our manifestations.

Ramtha has said that you always create your common thoughts into reality. Common thought means that you have an existing neuronet that is already constructed that will produce this reality by simply thinking of it. Another way to create reality is to repeat a statement or focus on a picture over and over until it becomes common to us. If you do this enough, it will become very common to you. The moment it is a common thought or picture is the moment it has been wired neurologically in your brain. Once it is neurologically wired, the Observer will observe that concept into your reality.

Ramtha is a master at saying the same thing in a thousand different ways until everyone in his audience understands the concept. He will teach us a discipline, and when we can do the discipline with consistent success he evolves the discipline. This is the reason why some people think that he contradicts himself. However, I have been able to watch the beginning students in our school for the past eighteen years. They are taught the most advanced disciplines in the school and they accomplish in eight days what it took the advanced students fifteen years to accomplish. They are the beneficiaries of those who were taught before them.

"You're only as young
as the last time
you changed your mind."

Timothy Leary

American Educator

Chapter 19

GOD ONLY KNOWS WHAT YOU KNOW

"What does the statement 'God only knows what you know' mean?"

We often think that God has all the answers and in one aspect this is absolutely true. Yet ninety-nine percent of the time when we use the neocortex, our personality, we only have access to our accumulated knowledge. For all practical purposes, we only know what God (ourself) knows.

With greater knowledge we have greater options and choices. The story of my five-year-old son with the $1,000,000 bill is a great example that the choices we have are correlated to the amount of knowledge we have. In the school we are hungry for knowledge.

"Many great works were created in poetry form. Do you think Dante's works were inspired by his meeting a guide or master? Could he have been inspired by divine intervention?"

I think many people were inspired by divine intervention. Remember how Elizabeth I was able to defeat the great Spanish Armada when she defied the Pope and supported the Church of England. However, I do not think Dante was inspired. He has frightened too many people with his *Inferno*, a rendition of hell, since the year he created that work. He was more fanatical than inspired. Inspiration always renders a lofty interpretation of life, and his work was far from that.

Others have been obviously inspired. J.R.R. Tolkien and his work on Middle-earth was his final thesis as a 32nd-degree Mason, according to Ramtha. Handel was required to write music that would create a five-pointed star as a hologram in the brain of those who listened to his music. His famous piece, *Messiah*, was his final assignment as an initiate in a secret society. There are many more who have been inspired by divine intervention. As we have learned in our school, we have the capacity to provide our own divine intervention by accessing the subconscious mind, the home of the Observer. We are always hooked up to the quantum field, or the mind of God as it was called in ancient times. If we can learn how to package information properly and present it in a specific way, then we always have access to divine intervention.

"Do we know more than we remember?"

Ramtha calls us "forgotten Gods," and that's a lot of forgetting. When students come to school and hear Ramtha's message, most of them say they have always known that what he was teaching was the truth but they had forgotten that they knew it. If we can learn to use our brain properly and process new knowledge, then we can begin to remember what it is we have always known, and that is part of what we do in our school. The moment you begin to become who you are, you begin to remember who you have always been. The school peels away the layers of image so that the becoming can be experienced.

"Why does Ramtha talk so differently from his earlier teachings?"

In the early days of his teachings as I recall him saying, he used the English language with the action words or verbs at the beginning of a sentence because they had more power in that form of communication. He used phrases such as "as it were indeed" and "that which is termed" to place additional emphasis on certain words or concepts. However, he has changed because people can understand him better with a more modern syntax. He is a God who continues to find better ways to get his message across. He can see how his choice of words and the order that he communicates them affect the pictures that his students are processing and the effect his language has on their brains. If he can get his students to process holograms of thoughts that he is communicating, then he knows that they will create that reality. His language and style of delivery have been an evolution based on effective communication.

"Is Ramtha the only teacher right now or are there others?"

There may be other teachers; however, there are no other teachers who are presenting this knowledge in a public forum for common people. If there were such a place, I think I would have heard about it in my travels. Most evolved beings who reach a level of enlightenment that would earn them the right to teach others seem to have little interest in students. These enlightened beings are interested in their own evolution and that is their singular focus. Occasionally these advanced masters would take on several students in order for the knowledge to continue. In contrast, many gurus or teachers who have not reached this level of enlightenment seem to want to have students. They seem to be more gratified with teaching students than accelerating their own evolution. I saw this in India in 1997 when I visited several ashrams. I believe our school is the most accessible place for common people to be taught ancient knowledge with the disciplines necessary to experience that knowledge into personal wisdom.

"In reference to beings living in advanced civilizations in other parts of the cosmos, do they need a teacher like Ramtha to evolve? Why have they not ascended if they are

more advanced? What would he teach them?"

I would imagine that he would teach them the next level of knowledge necessary for them to continue evolving. I once asked Ramtha when he knew what he was going to teach an audience. He told me it takes him several seconds to scan the audience to know what knowledge they would be requiring to evolve. I think he still does that with each group and each teaching session. Ramtha does have another school. It is located in the twenty-third universe. He said that he has over thirty million students attending that school.

"If observing something alters that thing totally and radically from something possible to something certain, which field of consciousness is doing the observing?"

The Observer is primary consciousness and it is looking at the thoughts of secondary consciousness. The field of consciousness and energy will be frequency specific with the level of thought that is being activated through the neuronet. We have seven levels of consciousness and energy, and the level necessary to endorse an idea from its probability into its certainty will depend on the idea.

The question Einstein asked as to whether the light on his bicycle would go on if he were traveling at the speed of light was an idea that could be facilitated by the frequency and the information in the light band of the light spectrum. That is the level of consciousness and energy that could provide the information needed for his famous theory of special relativity. We have a brain that is sophisticated enough to facilitate all seven levels of consciousness and energy to create any reality that we have the mind to construct as a model of thought.

Primary consciousness is the Father, the unconditional love of God. Whatever we are dreaming, this consciousness will manifest. Secondary consciousness is the dreamer, the son, and the traveler in space and time that is fulfilling the original mandate to make known the unknown. These two components

"Do I contradict myself?
Very well, then I contradict myself,
I am large, I contain multitudes."

Walt Whitman
American Poet

Chapter 20

Gurus

"When people hear the words School of Enlightenment, they think that there must be a guru. So what is the difference between a guru and a master teacher?"

It is so important to make the distinction. I have been to India and I have been with gurus in India and in the United States, and I am now under the tutelage of a Master Teacher. There is a vast difference between the two teachers.

Gurus usually utilize the energy of their students to stay empowered. Without the student, there is no guru. Therefore job security depends on enrollment and retention. I am certain there are master teachers who appear to be gurus, but the function of the master teacher is radically different than that of a guru.

A master teacher wants to empower the student, and once under their tutelage he or she will use any means necessary to evolve the student. A master teacher will not seek worship in any form and often will release any student that tends toward worship. A guru, at least those I have seen and those gurus with which I was familiar, insisted on being worshiped. Remember, with a guru, enrollment must be maintained. With a master teacher, there are no rules.

One of the general presumptions of a disciple studying under a guru was that the guru would take on the student's karma. As a disciple, you renounced your worldly goods or gave them to the ashram (preferably), stayed on the premises, and attended the spiritual teachings. This was one of the principal understandings of the guru/disciple relationship, and for so many people looking for a spiritual journey without responsibility this was a great marketing strategy.

However, no self-respecting master would ever rob his students from owning their karma through the teaching of knowledge and the unpredictable experiences of life. There are many additional differences. A master teacher is completely self-sufficient; therefore it is a sacrifice for them to teach. For a guru, it is more like a career move because power and its intoxication are very seductive.

I have yet to see or hear of a guru who has defied death, so they have very little to offer an incarnating Spirit. When a guru can teach a student how to become physically immortal because they have done that for themselves, or at least how to extend their students' lives by one hundred years or more, then they have earned the right to be heard.

"Is Sai Baba one of these enlightened teachers?"

When I visited Sai Baba's ashram in India, it was a very suppressive and strictly regulated organization. Joy was nowhere to be found among the Sai Baba staff. He was so old that he could hardly walk. I do not consider this an enlightened characteristic. He has been accused of molesting some of the younger boys. One European student in our school confirmed this, as he was one of those younger boys a few years ago. So how enlightened can one be who needs so much attention and abusive satisfaction? It is always difficult to know the level of enlightenment among the students of an organization if they never have to demonstrate their skills. At our school we are required to be tested on a consistent basis to demonstrate our level of mastery. In our school if you are not progressing as a master, you are not progressed as a leader.

"According to Ramtha, he reached enlightenment at

an early age. Why did he continue to march and conquer people throughout the remainder of his life?"

He was run through with a sword at twenty-four years old and convalesced on a rock until he was thirty-one. He was once asked, "What was it that you did for the remainder of your life," and he said, "I was owning my past."

His battle strategy changed dramatically after he became enlightened. He was able to conquer his enemy without using swords. He would march on his enemy in the early morning and with burnished copper shields he was able to blind the enemy with the bright reflection of the sun and capture them without spilling blood. In his enlightenment he had to use a greater mind to conquer his enemies. This new strategy was the result of his understanding that anyone he killed, he was only postponing his meeting them at a later date.

"The main failure of education is that it has not prepared people to comprehend matters concerning human destiny."

Norman Cousins
American Physician

Chapter 21

OPPORTUNITIES

"Can you describe an ideal day in a student's life, how to begin and end the day, and what one is supposed to do during the day? Can you give an overview for those who may be interested in the school?"

A master always creates his day, as Ramtha has told us. If you understand that thoughts create reality, then you would want to visualize your day before actually engaging it. This is not much different than being prepared for any presentation. You would not go into an important business meeting without being prepared. Well, every day is that important to a sincere student of the Great Work.

We know from science that quantum physicists know that all time exists simultaneously. Therefore in the morning before getting out of bed you create your day as if it were happening in that very moment. In scientific understanding, it is happening that very moment and you will experience it in the linear time-flow called the remainder of the day. So the morning is very important to influencing the experiences of your day.

After having created your day, you pause. You are now allowing your midbrain that has access to your immediate future an opportunity to send you the images and impressions of those activities that have the highest probability of manifesting that day. These impressions can include phone calls, unusual meetings, and even emergencies. If you pay attention to these impressions, you will get a preview of your day. If you are in the school, you will have learned how to dissolve any impression that you choose not to experience or, at the very least, be prepared for it. These midbrain impressions, after having created your day, have saved more than one student's life.

Therefore your day is to be lived according to your creation that day and the manifestations you have been focusing on. If you can learn to live in the moment, then doors of opportunity will open to you and magic will abound. This is our practice and discipline during the day.

In the evenings as we prepare to go to sleep, we have two objectives as a student. The first is to communicate to the subconscious mind regarding those areas of the body that need restoration. The second task is to assure our personality that we will be traveling that evening and we are requesting that this part of the brain track the experience for our conscious understanding. In addition, we continue to tell that part of our brain that we will return and there is no need for concern. Now we have programmed our subconscious mind to heal the body and we have notified our personality that we will be attending night school for our continuing education.

We must assure the neocortex that we will be returning. The neocortex becomes alarmed anytime it becomes aware that consciousness has transcended the physical body and is occupying a higher state of awareness. To the brain this is extremely fearful because it equates leaving the physical body with death. Have you ever awoken frightened and short of breath? This is the brain realizing that you were not home. It panics and dials 911.

We use this time at night to experience worlds not generally available to us during our busy days. We have six other kingdoms to investigate. The early morning and the evenings just before going to sleep are the times during the day when we can most easily work with the subconscious mind. We are highly vulnerable to suggestion at these times during which the neocortex is least active.

"I believe that levitation and bilocation are in my future through application, but what is foremost on my mind is handling this earthly life and being able to enjoy the human pleasures of fabulous wealth and a life partner. Am I dreaming way too small?"

No, nobody successfully dreams of levitation and bilocation while their refrigerator is empty or their heart is unfulfilled. Until you create these earthly pleasures you will always wonder what it would be like to have them, and that will stand in your way of creating a greater reality. Once you have owned the dreams of wealth, partnership, family, and material possessions, you will be free to dream the dreams of a greater reality, but not until then.

"What is the most difficult part of the spiritual journey?"

All of it until you make it the most important aspect of yourself. Until then it is a battle between the world of social consciousness and the world of making known the unknown. Most people have a regular life and a spiritual life. In truth, we are always living a spiritual life, for who we are is Spirit housed in a physical body. So we cannot live anything but a spiritual life. However, the most difficult part is sacrificing everything we have been taught for the need to be successful in this world and completely depending upon the God within to move us in directions we would not take on our own. This says that we know that the part of us that is best suited to guide us has not been in charge for a long time, and you are requesting a reorganization of leadership in your life. For those who have made this decision, it is the most exhilarating, challenging, and oftentimes the most frightening decision that was ever made. And this new journey will often include being successful in the world. However, there is one absolute guarantee and that is that your life will never be boring again. This is the quintessential decision that is made by students on their journey to mastership.

Most people want to get all the information necessary to

make that kind of radical move, but the part of the brain being used to make that assessment does not have the knowledge necessary to justify that move. It is a "leap of faith" that must be taken. It is only after the leap that the next step appears. It never appears before the leap. That is the beauty and reward of taking risks.

"What is the way I can refine creating my day? I am not experiencing a shift. I know that it can work. It just doesn't seem to be working for me."

It will not work for you or anyone else as long as you do not move to a new neuronet that is frequency-specific to the day you want to create. If we try to create a new day from the same old mind we have today, it will not produce the new experience. We can only produce the new day from the new mind that sets the template for those experiences. You will have to come to school to learn this properly. We are learning to have thoughts that the Observer can collapse that correlate to the new day we want to create. You must already become the person who will experience the day you want to create. When I create my day, I reach a state of excitement and hope before I begin to say what it is I want to experience that day. If you try to Create Your Day^{SM} before you reach a new level of passion and expectation, you will not create a new and different day. You will create the day that is consistent with that mind that is creating a template of your normal day.

You become excited because the new neuronet is sending a new message to the cells and they are responding to this new frequency. Now is the time to create the day from the mind of those new possibilities. We do that in one of the newest disciplines we have been taught in the school. It is so powerful that you can reinvent yourself and its complete history in a moment.

I used this discipline to stop smoking. It took less than a minute and I was so thoroughly changed that I did not recognize the pack of cigarettes in my room. I called one of the other staff members who smoked the same kind of cigarettes and I told them that they had left their cigarettes in my room. They came over and kindly got their cigarettes. That was reinventing myself in a dramatic way. No one asked me for a cigarette, a light, or missed me in the smoking area. It was as if no one knew I had ever smoked, even those who I had smoked with just the day before. That is changing yourself that is accompanied with a history that has always been that way. If you change yourself this way, you will have little or no memory of the way you were before the change. I never remember that I smoked at one point in my life except when I tell this story. Then I remember, but it is like it was a dream. I have never once had the urge to smoke again. If you learn to reinvent yourself in this same way, you will have found a key to instant manifestation.

"Can you explain all the biological processes that take place in the body when you are doing C&E®?"

I don't know all of the processes that are taking place, but I know several that are important. The brain gets oxygenated and nourished by the increased circulation of the spinal fluid. In the spinal fluid are ions that create a field effect, which creates a phosphorescent effect that anesthetizes the brain. This is necessary in order to introduce a new idea without the automatic program of objection. The second most important function is that this breath technique produces a large amount of proteins in the bloodstream. As nutritionists have come to understand in the last few years, all diseases live in an acid environment. These proteins create an alkaline environment in the body, a natural defense to disease. The C&E® breath naturally detoxifies the body and restores it to a greater level of health.

"We do all our disciplines but we do not concentrate on any one of them. Is this the most effective way to increase our ability to focus, or should we pick one and become the master of it?"

I have watched students in our school who are particularly good at one of the disciplines and they are generally good at others as well. However, they seem to have a preference for one or two. I would suggest that if you can master one of the disciplines, the discipline of your choice, you will become better at the others because they require the same kind of focus to be successful. When I was a long-distance runner and I began to cross-train with swimming and bicycling, my times for long-distance running improved. It may be the same with the disciplines.

I have seen students in our school who were not good at one discipline, but after mastering a discipline of their choice they became very good at those they had difficulty with in the past. The advantage of mastering the discipline of your choice is that you will be motivated to work on it more than a discipline in which you are not as interested.

The moment Master of Music became a master of the cards, she began to consistently find her card in the name-field. Before developing her focus to see through cards, however, she had a great difficulty in finding her card in the field. That has all changed with her new mastery. If you focus on one of the disciplines with the absolute intention of being its master, you will develop a neuronet that can be transferred to any of the other disciplines. It can be more difficult to see dramatic results when you are working on five or six disciplines at the same time. Pick a discipline that you are passionate about and master its challenge.

"What is the secret to focus?"

Practice with a true desire to change your life. I have been working on Fieldwork^SM lately as my discipline of choice. For the first time I have come to understand that there is a methodology to it. If I can only see my card for a few seconds at a time, then I know that I am not in the correct neuronet that is frequency specific with that potential reality. Now all I have to do is continue to insist that my brain see that image over and over.

Eventually we move to the part of the brain that is frequency specific with that potential. I become analogical and I find my card. My greatest realization in doing Fieldwork[SM] lately is that I know that I can have anything I want as long as I am willing to sacrifice the time it takes to create it. Some things I am willing to sacrifice the time for and at this point some things I am not.

"How do we stop boredom?"

Stop doing whatever it is you think is creating your boredom. Within moments of quitting, you will no longer be bored. Your boredom will be replaced with the anxiety of what will you do now? The beauty of this is that you can create anything since you are in free space. Boredom, as Ramtha has often said, is a sign from the soul that you have owned what it is you are doing and that it is time to do something different.

"If all created realities have benefits for the creator, what are some of the benefits for those who are ill?"

This is an excellent question because it seems preposterous to think that someone who is ill would prefer that condition to health, but that is the way it is. Remember the story of the children of the Bronx? That is just as preposterous.

The greatest benefit to illness is sympathetic attention. For many human beings there is an overwhelming need for this emotion, which often translates into a form of love. The amount of attention created by one who is ill is often far greater than what one could create in health. This situation alone can perpetuate an illness for a long time.

All illnesses are generally blamed on some circumstance or situation outside the person who is affected. The first step to recovery, assuming this is what the person wants, is to take one-hundred-percent responsibility for creating this condition. That is what a master would do, and it will take a masterful mind to heal an ill body.

"Do you think thoughts can affect the acne of the skin even after prolonged stress?"

It was thoughts and attitudes that created the condition in the first place, so it will be thoughts that will clear it up. Consciousness and energy creates the nature of reality in all cases, and skin conditions are not the exception to the rule.

"It is understood that cancer activates for a reason. I have recently activated breast cancer. What is the attitude behind this? Is it self-doubt?"

It is not self-doubt. Hate is the attitude behind cancer. The moment any of us begins to dislike our bodies for any reason, the body begins its slow demise into disease. Breast cancer is almost epidemic with women because they think that they have to please people in order to be considered valuable. A woman's body is often used to ensure that outcome of acceptance. Most women feel a deep frustration for having to survive this way, and frustration over time will lead to hatred.

Cancer cells are immortal. They have the fortitude and determination to complete their task. They will destroy the other cells in the body by following the orders of the attitude. Conventional cancer treatment does not correct the attitudes in a person. The respect for life and the opportunity to sincerely prioritize one's life is what slows the process down. There was a statistic a few years ago that stated that cancer patients who had no treatments lived seven years longer than those who took the conventional treatments. The first step, however, to a full recovery is taking responsibility for the creation. When that is done, the effects of being victimized by the disease are no longer apparent and the body can begin to repair. Once an understanding of the attitude is known, and a sincere change is made, the disease begins to dissipate because the signals being sent to the cells are no longer the same signals as before. The body heals when the attitude is forgiven. The transformation from hatred to humble is a life-sustaining attitude and the body must now respond to that new attitude. Remember the Hawaiian doctor and his power of healing. When he forgave the part of himself that allowed those reflections to exist in his environment, they disappeared.

"A great many people think
that they are thinking when they are merely
rearranging their prejudices."

William James
American Philosopher

Chapter 22

SEX, LOVE, AND RUMORS

"Regarding emotional needs, in particular sexual orgasm, there is not always the good feeling afterwards. There is something lacking, something missing. I continue to pursue this climax after climax. How do you find the middle ground between indulgence and abstinence?"

If it is your intent to become balanced in this area of the middle ground, you will find it. The reason there is something lacking in your sexual activity is because it has become a routine and you have lost the art of being in the moment with your partner.

If sexual activity becomes a need rather than a creative endeavor, then you are subject to the same rules as any other addiction. Once this emotional addiction is understood — and some of the first signs will be the lacking of those same "good feelings" that generally accompanied this act — then you can make a different choice. However, the most powerful experience with another person will always require that you are being in the moment with that person and that state of mind is never in need.

If you can approach this moment of intimate sharing as new each and every time, you will find the middle path between indulgence and abstinence. A great meal consciously prepared and aesthetically presented with a mind for detail requires much less food to fill a person's stomach.

"Love is a word that is mentioned a lot and very misunderstood. I remember reading about the seven levels of reality, and when Ramtha referred to the fourth and the fifth he said that the fourth was love felt and the fifth was love given. Please explain love in this context."

The fourth level of consciousness and energy is the ultraviolet-blue frequency. This is the frequency above and faster than the light. It is the first environment above the light that is without polarization. Polarization happened at the light as energy became slow on its descent and split into positive and negative charges, the very elements needed for electricity. The fourth level is called unconditional love because it is without polarization. Polarization has to do with opposites: good and bad, high and low, trust and betrayal, etc. Therefore love defined at this level of reality means that it is unconditional and without judgment or conclusion. It is a unified field. To remain at this level of consciousness and energy is to say that the master is born.

The fourth seal is precisely the destination of all our humanly efforts in becoming transcendent. We are here to conquer ourselves. What we are conquering are our emotional responses to the circumstances in our life. Once we are no longer bothered by what bothered us before, we have moved into the fourth seal and the mind-set of being nonjudgmental. We are unified. So there is a greater understanding of those still engaged in the human drama of emotions and yet they are not judged for those behaviors because it is understood that they are still in the middle of the experience.

In this level of reality, there is a patience that transcends all understanding because this reality of unconditional love is not associated with time but rather an eternal aspect of ourselves that is beyond time. The reward of living in this level of frequency is that neither death, age, nor disease may manifest, for these are the attitudes of the first three seals, and the radiant frequency of unconditional love is transcendent of these attitudes.

The fifth seal is said to be love given. Ramtha has told us that the fifth seal is the seal of truth, and of course truth is always love given.

In contrast to that, the love that we are more familiar with is based on need in the lower three seals. It is based always on survival. The reason we seek it is because we are unfulfilled within ourselves so we look outside ourselves to fill that emptiness. The irony is that nothing outside ourselves will fill that emptiness as a permanent condition. The only strategy people know is to move from partner to partner or suffer the experience of being unfulfilled. It takes a rare person to insist on fulfilling themselves by depending upon their own resources. However, these are the exact people who have the most to give because they are satisfied within themselves.

"I have been taking hypnotherapy classes for a year and there are some similarities in these classes and what you have been talking about. I am a freshman in college and would like to know how to introduce Ramtha's teachings to my associates without seeming to force the information on them. Secondly, what advice do you have for the mistake I recently made and now I am trying to get over a broken heart?"

If you use science as a way to introduce Ramtha to your college associates, you will be giving them information that is already in an acceptable form. Once they realize the genius of the mind of Ramtha, they will do the inquiring and you can answer the questions. Once a person has asked you a question, they have given you permission to elaborate and explain.

In our school, there are no mistakes. There is only experience, learning, and becoming wiser as a result of that experience. A broken heart is feedback that you will need to do it differently next time. If you can continue to modify your life and learn from your experiences, you will continue to become wiser and wiser. That is the process of evolution, the true spiritual journey.

Love is always given unconditionally without the need or expectation of it being reciprocated. There are no broken hearts in love. There is always a broken heart in need. When we can see need for what it is, then we will be in a position to change. If we keep insisting that love hurts, then we will always remain a victim. The beauty of need and its emotional pain is that it will always be healed by time, and we can always learn about ourself in the process. All experience has purposeful good as a by-product if you are willing to see it from that vantage. You should never be so devastated that you are afraid to try again. Life is a wonderful and risky adventure if you are courageous enough to explore its possibilities.

Relationships are one of the greatest opportunities to see where you compromise your own needs, feel insecure within yourself, or have the experience of uncontrolled dependence. However, if each new adventure is built upon the experience and the wisdom of the previous experiences, then your life can only continue to get better because you continue to get better. If we can bless the difficult experiences as well as celebrate those experiences that bring us joy, then we have become more noble in our being and we deserve the passion that comes with fearless participation in life.

"Today a young man under the influence of LSD realized that all matter is energy condensed to a slow vibration and that we are all one consciousness experiencing ourselves objectively. He realized that there is no such thing as death and that life is simply a dream in which we are an imagination of ourselves. This person is of the opinion that drugs that grow naturally like psychedelic mushrooms and marijuana were put here by God to speed up our evolution. Can you comment?"

Ramtha has said that there is no drug that is more powerful in assisting us in human evolution than our brain. The only thing put here by God to speed up our evolution is the knowledge of evolution and a brain necessary to process that information into experience. Marijuana was put here by a compassionate God to help animals curb the pain that comes as a result of vicious attacks. It grew naturally so that it could be easily found by animals that needed its medicinal effects. It was never intended as a tool for personal evolution. Our brain can facilitate all seven levels of frequency, and that cannot be duplicated by any drug.

Drugs are an easy path used by unenlightened people because they only require consuming. Drugs have the effect of misfiring the neuronets in the brain and this has often been translated as cosmic experiences because they can be so bizarre. They will not enlighten an individual. They will destroy an individual's ability to create reality because they become too lethargic to make the effort. Enlightenment and its evolution is the processing of new information into new experience. Doing something new and different is a transcendent experience. While all drugs do contain information, do you really want to consume the information that was created to help an animal numb its pain after a vicious attack? There are greater realities to experience.

"Twice in my life I have experienced the effects of a super endorphin. In both cases the effect lasted for several days. It sounds like the runner's high that is talked about and is quite addictive. When C&E® is done properly, are endorphins released or inhibited from being released? I thought that powerful chemicals were bad for the body."

I was a long-distance runner for many years and I know the feeling of these chemicals being released and the effects of the withdrawal when I didn't run. Any chemistry that requires us to do something for its release will become a habit, and all habits are detrimental to the body. C&E® is not addictive. You do not wake up in the morning and feel the need to create chemicals in the body that will help you function better. You do C&E® in the morning to prepare your brain to create a specific intent for the day. That is being the master of the day and not letting the day be the master of you. If endorphins are released in the brain during C&E®, then they are a natural effect of moving energy in the body and into the brain. The C&E® breath technique will naturally detoxify the body by producing large amounts of protein in the bloodstream. As all disease in the body lives in an acid environment, this breath technique produces an alkaline environment in which disease cannot live. It is that beneficial to the body.

"How do you attract positive, healthy relationships? I find the dating scene in my thirties a nightmare."

Become exactly who you want to attract. Until you change, you will continue attracting the same quality of person which you have already stated is a nightmare. It is a nightmare because you have not changed to reflect a different aspect of yourself in another. You will always attract what is frequency specific to yourself. Out of your mind come the people, places, things, times, and events that make up your environment. Only when you change will the people in your environment change.

"I am a female. When we come from the fourth plane and descend into the Hertzian plane, do we continuously evolve as females unless we choose to be crossovers?"

We can stay one gender the entire journey of evolution. However, if the soul and the Spirit decide that you would gain greater understanding by becoming a crossover, a male energy in a female body or a female energy in a male body, then that choice is made and you have the crossover experience. The soul has an agenda based on what it is that you have yet to own, and if the crossover experience will place you in a genetic body with a greater opportunity to own what is yet to be owned, then that is the decision made for the next incarnation.

I have heard Ramtha talking about genders that abuse the other gender, either physically or mentally, and in the next experience they will cross over to gain the wisdom of their former acts of abuse. There is a wise and just system of equality being rendered to each of us by a greater intelligence, and it is always working toward our evolutionary benefit. We don't really choose to be a certain gender in the strict sense of "I think I'll be a female this time around." It is more like "Does becoming a crossover give me the greatest opportunity to evolve spiritually?"

Many men, having seen the atrocities of war and losing fathers and brothers in battle, would often incarnate as women so that they could avoid those same possible atrocities in their next life. Ramtha told us that many men would do that to avoid going to war. Again, you are given the body and the persuasive genetics of that body to enhance your chances of owning aspects of your personality that you have yet to own.

Any habit or emotional response that is automatic is an aspect of one's personality that needs to be owned. You can look at your own life and see where you are out of control, meaning that you always respond in the same way to a specific circumstance. Any area of your life in which you have an automatic response means that you are not acting out of choice. Owning, in its simplest terms, means that what bothered you before no longer bothers you now or how you automatically responded before can be responded to in a different way. It is the genetics encoded in the DNA of every cell in our body that compels us to continue to respond automatically. This is what must be owned. It is the process of spiritual evolution. The offspring of one who owns a specific emotion will not have that emotion encoded in its DNA. It will not be passed on in genetic form to the children.

Our children are our greatest opportunity to evolve because they represent genetically what it is we have yet to own. This can explain why we are so frustrated with them at times. They are a painful mirror of what we ourselves must overcome. However, with knowledge we can look at our children as the greatest mirror of what we must own within ourself. When Ramtha was telling me that loving my first son would actually be the process of loving myself, he was right. Our children are the exact reflections of what we pass on genetically that was not yet owned. They might as well be wearing a T-shirt that says, "I am what you have yet to own. Hello!"

"I would enjoy attending a Beginning Retreat but my husband is against it. I know if he understood more about it that he wouldn't be afraid for me to visit. Do you have information for family members to give them the truth about the great knowledge available at Ramtha's School of Enlightenment? If he were not dreaming up stories or listening to far-fetched rumors, he would be much more apt to become a student himself. Could you help me out with an approach that would be educational and factual?"

On the one hand I am happy that your husband is cautious. If his intent is to protect you from getting involved in a cult or a tenuous organization that is mostly interested in producing profits, then he has every right to his opinion and with conviction. If, however, he is afraid that you will get knowledge and change into something else, thus changing your relationship with him, then that is a completely different matter.

RSE is an established school with students attending from over twenty-five different countries. The school is so unique that not one student in over twenty years has ever compared the school to any other organization or movement.

RSE is currently "the most innovative laboratory for the human mind." That sounds very biased, but it wasn't I who said that. It was a tenured professor, Dr. Joseph Bettis, director of the Northwest Research Group, who was one of twelve scholars who studied the school for over two years.

When a school depends on knowledge and experience as fundamental to its curriculum, it is a challenge to communicate the effectiveness of these components to the world at large. If you go to the ramtha.com Web site, it contains information about the school, its scheduled events, the costs, and general information helpful to attending a Beginning Retreat. In addition, there are video extracts that give a taste of the school and show some of our advanced students doing remarkable things with their minds. If this does not inspire someone to want to know more, then they need more information until that moment comes. However, the greatest inspiration to another person will be to see someone they know become an inspired, self-assured, and knowledgeable person.

"Is it possible to progress and evolve by reading Ramtha books without attending an event?"

Of course, everything is possible. We know that from our understanding of quantum physics. However, if you want to optimize the time working on yourself, then having an environment that is dedicated to personal evolution is highly suggested. What sets this school apart from most organizations is that nothing is accepted as truth unless it is personally experienced. Experience is difficult to get out of books, as they are generally not designed for that specific application. Books are designed for knowledge, the first ingredient for evolving. Now you can take this knowledge and with the proper discipline experience the philosophy as personal truth and wisdom. Our school is designed to provide a direct experience of its philosophy.

We don't evolve through reading unless it moves us to an action that results in or provides us with an experience. If a book can do that, then it has the power of initiation that is necessary for evolution.

"How is your school different from Scientology? And are there similarities?"

I am in a good position to answer this question as I studied the Scientology technology for several years. It has one similarity that has to do with owning the emotional responses that we habitually express. Both organizations work diligently to erase these automatic responses. Both organizations are successful in this. With this exception, the organizations are vastly different. The marketing strategies are different, the costs are vastly divergent, at RSE you are free to continue studying other disciplines, and you do not pledge allegiance to our school.

Ramtha's School of Enlightenment is very specific in its study of the brain and the proper use of the brain in creating reality. I know of no other organization that knows this knowledge. RSE has the most effective healing techniques that are available, and no organization has this knowledge. The school's philosophy and its disciplines were brought here by a teacher who has owned the human experience. The school is unique.

"Can you talk about the sacred sites? Are there any? Ramtha has mentioned that Stonehenge was simply a landing platform for UFOs. What's the truth?"

There is a lot of information about sites constructed on leylines that emit energy vortexes and sites that have reputations for all sorts of phenomena. My answer is going to be disappointing to those people who love the mystique of a sacred site or empower it with their own belief. However, Ramtha has told us that the most perfect temple is the human body because it houses a Spirit. This temple or sacred site certainly shines with a divine legacy and transcendent potentials that clearly outshine any abandoned sacred site.

On a tour of England and Ireland several years ago, I was able to visit Stonehenge and Avebury on the first of two visits to those sacred sites. I was shocked and surprised when we pulled up to Stonehenge. It is so small compared to its reputation and the way in which it is photographed. My mind had exaggerated a story and mystique about this site and it had become larger than life itself. Ramtha has a way of demystifying our conceptions of history and the way we tend to fabricate the conditions of that time. When he said it had nothing to do with a celestial calendar but was rather a landing platform for crafts, I laughed at how we can embellish something we know nothing about. When I saw the stones of Avebury, I laughed so hard I embarrassed myself, as I was on a group tour. I told a friend of mine who accompanied me on the trip that I had seen stones this big in the Bald Hill area, about fifteen minutes from the school. We both realized how big something can become without knowledge and a little agreement among so-called experts.

On my second trip to Avebury at a popular pub, I asked some of the locals about the crop circles that were prevalent in this part of England. In fact, there were two fresh circles within walking distance, and I thoroughly investigated the largest one. However, my conversation with a very hip, local man set the record straight. He told me that some of the circles were considered art and done by some of the locals in the area. He told me how they accomplished it, that it was a very organized and efficient operation, and that the circle had to be completed during the night before the sun came up the next morning. Now I was impressed. I wasn't impressed that a UFO, using musical frequency, carved exact symbols and elaborate images in the crops but that a group of human beings could create a huge, dimensionally perfect crop circle using plywood alone as its high-tech tool. That was certainly an accomplishment.

Are some of the crop circles done by UFO's sending a message? Probably, but those in Avebury had a practical explanation, and as the local told me, it wasn't a surprise that they appeared every summer during the high tourist season.

What is important is that the sacred monuments and sites point to a greater truth. The cathedrals in Europe remind us of the Observer effect in creating reality, and this knowledge was built into great stone edifices. Once again, the human body is the greatest temple ever created and houses our Spirit, a testament to a greater truth.

"Has Ramtha talked about the Indigo children?"

He has not talked about them in any specific way. However, I went to a three-day conference in Ashland, Oregon that promoted these children as being very special with very special gifts. The Indigo children at this conference seemed no more special than any other children their age. In fact, they acted as silly as most teenagers do when they are introduced as being special. If they had any gifts, they were cleverly hidden that weekend.

"Do the phases of the moon affect humanity in any

shape or form? My sister is a pagan and holds her rituals on certain phases of the moon. There is also a moon planting guide for vegetables. Is there any truth in it?"

It has all the truth that one wants to accept. There is personal truth in everything that has been experienced. However, whether these are universal truths for everyone is another issue. Ancient rituals were often scheduled according to the phases of the moon. There must have been some reason, practical or superstitious, for using the moon as a reference. Rituals are used to create an environment to enhance the participant's expectation of an experience.

It is believed that planting your garden on a waxing moon has a beneficial effect on its eventual production. However, the real truth is that we often use symbols, archetypes, pagan rituals, astrology, numerology, and other tools to give ourselves permission to create the results we want and could produce without those tools. The church has maintained a very successful business with middlemen. When we come to understand who we are, we put away those intermediary substitutes of permission and create reality using the tools we have inherent within us. Many people will tell you that they believe that God is within, but very few act as if that is so.

However, the most sacred site I have seen and visited is the Guinness Brewery complex in Dublin, Ireland. It was leased in the 1400s for nine thousand years at an annual cost of twenty-five sterling pounds. The original owner had a vision of the future that has guaranteed his employment for the next nine millennium. This is the vision and the mind of a master.

"Nobody realizes that some people
expend tremendous energy
merely to be normal."

Albert Camus
French Philosopher

Chapter 23

Soulmates and the Soul

"I grieve for my soulmate who meant so much to me in a former life but who comes to me this lifetime while spending most of his time with others. He only checks in with me on occasion. He will not live with me, as I so wish that he would. Can you explain this?"

The concept of soulmates has become a very romantic idea because very few people understand the origin or the function of soulmates. Soulmates came about when Gods, in the process of making known the unknown, moved into the frequency of the light. The realm of the light is polarized, having positively and negatively charged particles that interact. Soulmates are one being that split on their journey into the light, an agenda with two components to be experienced, creating a positive energy (male) and a negative energy (female). Positive and negative are charges, not evaluations. Both charges are equally needed in this environment for realization, procreation, and understanding.

Soulmates are mirror representations of each other, matter and antimatter. What you will see in a soulmate is the best and the worst of yourself. It is one of the most difficult paths to realization, but because of its nature of showing you everything you must own, it can be one of the fastest paths to self-realization.

Before yearning for what most people think will be the

romantic adventure of their life, be aware this adventure often turns out to be the most confusing and painful. This will always be true if there is not this understanding of the nature of soulmates on which to build the relationship.

Soulmate encounters can be reviewed during your contemplation time between one incarnation and another. Between each incarnation we use the time to map a lifetime that will give us the opportunities to resolve the main issues of emotion that we have yet to own. If we have a "need" to be with someone specific, then that is an unresolved emotion. Maybe your "soulmate" is playing that role for you so that you can bring this "need" to full understanding and resolution. If this emotional "need" is not resolved with the experiences of this lifetime, it will be a genetic prominence in your next incarnation. We continue this circle until we have mastered every limited human "need." We will know when this moment comes when we no longer look outside ourselves for anything.

"I would like to know when the individual soul became created. Does each individual soul have to go through all the levels of consciousness and energy, or does it already start at a high level of consciousness?"

To understand the definition and the function of the soul will answer this question. According to Ramtha, the soul was first created on the sixth level of experience. In making known the unknown, each of us as individuals began by experiencing the seventh level of reality until each of us asked the question, "There must be something more," and then we would expand into the next lowered level called the sixth plane. This is the journey of each God descending into a lowered frequency in order to continue making known the unknown. This continues all the way down to the Hertzian plane, the level of frequency that you and I are enjoying today. We call it the first plane. The soul was created on the sixth plane to remember an experience so that the individual did not repeat the same experience over and over without knowing it was in repetition. The soul became the "official" recorder housed within the body to record our experiences. Each of our individual souls has recorded all of our experiences since the inception of consciousness and energy, starting with making known the unknown in the seventh level of reality. The ancient symbol for the soul is a book and it was called the Book of Life.

There are no new souls or old souls. Each soul is the same age, beginning with the birthing of all beings when Point Zero contemplated itself and expanded as primary and secondary consciousness into the seventh plane as the first act of consciousness and energy.

The soul, in addition to recording all our experiences, serves another important function. Once we have reviewed what it is that we have owned in a life's experience and what it is we have yet to own on this journey, the soul creates an encoded intent that will be the template for our next incarnation and its set of genetics. These specific genetics will determine who becomes our parents and each of us will be born with the same emotional propensities that we have yet to own. Forget the justice systems around the world. This is the most complete justice system created, as it takes into account all of our yet-to-be-owned experiences. The importance of the soul remembering what each of us has experienced allows for this function of genetic selectivity for evolving incarnations. The soul does not judge one's experience. It simply reports the results and designs the genetics that will ensure that you get the opportunity to reexperience the same conditions that you have yet to master. The soul has been doing this for countless millenniums. It has a level of patience we call eternity, so it does not matter how many lifetimes it takes to own these experiences.

"I have read Ramtha's book on *Soulmates* twice. Could you please explain about soulmates? Do they reconnect after journeying back to the higher planes? Did Jesus have a soulmate, and who could it have been?"

Soulmates are a product of polarity. In the process of

involution while making known the unknown, the expansion of a nongendered entity is to become a positive or negative energy. This split happens at the light on the way down to our three-dimensional reality. We have the experience of being a male or a female, and our opposite-gendered partner is called our soulmate. Once we ascend into the fourth level of reality as a permanent evolution, we are transcendent of gender. Jesus, like everyone else, has a soulmate. The only person who was his equal polarity in his lifetime would have been Mary Magdalene. However, I do not know if she is his soulmate.

"Am I interpreting this correctly? We have a God that continually gives us what we think, a soul which is similar to a strict teacher with a ruler in her hand overseeing our behavior, and a Spirit who is like the electric company that continues to work even in the worst storm until the soul determines that this adventure is becoming so predictable that making known the unknown is no longer an option. This begins the demise of the body until it expires."

That is a very good description except for the role of the soul. Once there is conception, the soul's greatest function, encoding the DNA, has already been completed and for the most part it will remain relatively quiet.

However, it is more of a counselor than a strict teacher. In fact, it makes very few suggestions and only three times does it urge the person to take notice of those suggestions. Before puberty, during one's midlife, and in old age, the soul urges the person to remember who it is and what it has been mandated to do: to make known the unknown. The true spiritual journey is not being any specific way. It is having new experiences, and that will be different for each person. Other than those three times, it is relatively quiet. However, once you begin a conscious journey to become something greater than your genetics, the soul will take on a more active role. It will let you know when you do something that you know is not evolutionary. It has been called "bruising the soul" and you will feel an ache near your heart. This is the additional role that the soul plays with students wanting to evolve.

If you continue to learn and gain knowledge, then you extend your life accordingly so that you can experience what you have learned. The moment you make the decision, consciously or unconsciously, that you do not want to learn any more knowledge is the moment the soul begins to calculate the ending of this incarnation. This is why Ramtha has said, "No one dies on the march." No one dies while they are still learning, experiencing, and evolving.

In my Neighborhood Walk[SM] I continue to say, "And every day, every day, I seize the opportunity to own aspects of a fragmented personality that heretofore could only react with limited emotions to the circumstances of my life, and in this ownership what bothered me before, bothers me nevermore." I say this every day to stay consciously aware of my automatic reactions to certain circumstances. What I can own will have an immediate impact on my body, its power to rejuvenate itself, and the genetics of my DNA will be changed to enforce that rejuvenation. Old age is the result of not owning these emotions and we wear out the connections necessary for producing healthy cells.

"What makes a desert beautiful
is that somewhere it hides a well."

Antoine de Saint-Exupéry

French Novelist

Chapter 24

Suicide and Death

"Will you address the implications of suicide on the soul's journey? No, I am not contemplating it myself. Someone I know just recently made this choice."

Whenever Ramtha talked about suicide, he made one statement that he said was common to all suicides and that is that at the moment it is done, every individual realizes that it is a mistake. The reason it is a mistake is because they realize that there is no reprieve in the afterlife and that you take with you the same emotions that were so overwhelming in the previous life. In the next incarnation you are going to be genetically encoded by the soul to confront the same circumstances that led to your previous choice of suicide to see if you have become older and wiser through your life's experiences. Often the circumstances in the new life are even more intense to ensure the confrontation.

The true spiritual journey is resolving the issues of humanity that still bother you. And as Ramtha has recently said, "If you can learn to live on this planet, you can live anywhere."

It is never too late to change. It is important to remember again that the soul sends the body and brain messages of urgency three times in each incarnation. The first is before puberty when the soul knows that the energy of a young child is still receptive and can be influenced before the chemistry of adolescence runs its cascade of chemicals that override all messages from the soul. The soul is urging the child to remember its divinity and purpose, which is to own its emotions of limitation and its emotions of habit.

The second time that the soul can easily reach a person is during one's "midlife crisis." This is the time when most people have forgotten their dreams of youth and are maintaining an existence of a normal and predictable life. This midlife crisis is when people begin to question their own assumptions about life. It is during this window of opportunity that the soul sends its reminders of the purpose of life, to master the areas of your life in which you are not in control. Those are the areas in which we respond automatically to situations. We continue to be angry when things do not go our way, or we continually compare our circumstance in life to those we deem more successful, or we continue to be impatient. All of the automatic responses are simply programs in the brain that run automatically when stimulated by the environment.

I know that one of my automatic programs is frustration when I am occupied with a project and I am continually interrupted. I am now practicing patience while I build. I have rarely worked on any building project in which I did not swear at the tools or the building. I once extended my middle finger to a ledge of dirt that kept falling into my carefully dug hole. I yelled at the dirt and tried to explain to it that I was endeavoring to become self-sufficient and it was not cooperating. When I realized what I was doing, I laughed out loud. Finally I told the dirt that it could fall as much as it wanted and that I would no longer swear at it for giving in to gravity. The dirt never fell after that moment.

The third and last time that the soul has easy access to the person is in old age and just before death. When a person is beyond outrageous youth and beyond the need to impress anyone, they are open to urges from the soul. It is unfortunate that just when a person is in the best position to take advantage of knowledge that they are at the end of their life. It has been said that many people learn the most at the end of their life because they have the perspective of all their choices and the results of those choices on their life. They can finally see that what they had lived their whole life for might not have been as important or satisfying as the life they could have lived had they lived it for themselves.

"Everybody is a dreamer. How is it that we don't consciously dream about dying and yet there is an accident and someone dies?"

We have an agenda that we are born into that is genetically encoded in the body. As a result of this we are predisposed with certain emotional reactions that are based on these genetics. It is the design of evolution that we become greater than those reactions in becoming wise through our life's experiences. However, if we are living a life that disregards any interest or attempt at becoming greater than these propensities, then our God plans for us a wake-up call, or the Spirit and soul begin to design an ending of the body in order to begin the incarnating process again.

Many people think that doing something new with this brain is actually making known the unknown. It is only a new experience to this new brain. It is not making known the unknown to the soul. We can get caught up in thinking that a new business, a different career, a new partner, or a location move is making known the unknown. It is only new to this brain. The soul, however, is recording this familiar experience for the seven thousand and fourteenth time. If the soul can predict the outcome of this scenario, as it has been able to do over the past several hundred thousand years, it may opt to begin the dissolution of this physical experience.

We can have thoughts on a continuous basis that will eventually unfold in life. Remember my story of the person who watched the news on television every night. Even though it may not be a part of our conscious dreams, circumstances in our life are not accidents. They are the unfolding of conscious and unconscious thinking.

"Does the soul come into the first incarnation with an

already high level of consciousness?"

It does not come into an incarnation with a high level of consciousness. Where would it have received that experience separate from the being of which it is intimately a part? Each of us was created at the same time from Point Zero.

"What about human cloning and the ramifications to Spirit?"

I do not make a distinction between a cloned body and one that is produced in a more traditional method. A body has one magnificent purpose and that is to house the Spirit of an incarnating God. The DNA of a body and its genetic signature, cloned or not, will determine the Spirit that is housed in that temple. It does not seem to make a significant difference when the understanding is that we are not our bodies. They are temporary structures to allow us to interact with the environment. Therefore there are no ramifications to Spirit. It is not a moral issue because it is a functional aspect of a natural evolutionary process. The Spirit enters into the body during the nine months of gestation and feeds the cellular organism. It is the soul that has up to one year after birth to decide whether it will encase itself permanently within the body. The sudden infant death syndrome (SIDS) is a function of a soul that decides to vacate the body within the first year of birth. That has always been a medical mystery but can now be understood within this context.

Ramtha has told us some very interesting stories about the Pharaohs and the *Egyptian Book of the Dead*. That book is an instructional manual of what to do when a Pharaoh dies. He is instructed to go to Sirius, the Dog Star. One of the options was to wait until the technology of cloning became perfected and then clone the original body from the DNA and house yourself once again in that familiar glorious body of thousands of years ago. According to Ramtha, the DNA from Ramses II has already been extracted from his mummified body in the Cairo Museum, and Akhnaton has been cloned. Now you have the ancient Pharaoh living again in his genetic body with the wisdom gained from having lived in another space and time. Although I cannot verify this, it is certainly an interesting possibility, and maybe in the near future we will be able to see and hear the wisdom from an ancient Pharaoh who has the details of that lifetime that will fill in some of the missing gaps. Imagine what this will do for those who are curious or undecided about reincarnation. The ancient Egyptians were the greatest race in history because they had the most concentrated amount of the DNA passed on from the Gods, and as such the Pharaohs were the first to rule under the tutelage of the Gods. Their leadership was of the highest moral caliber and dedicated to the good of the civilization. It is a far cry from the leadership of today that is politically biased, corrupt, and opportunistic.

"We are students in the school and if we have the privilege to be with someone who is dying, what would you suggest we tell them?"

I would suggest that you tell them what you have been taught. If people know about the tunnel and the importance of getting into it, then you will have helped escort them to the next step. Not everyone knows about the tunnel or is willing to go toward it. I had the opportunity to tell my stepmother about the process of death and its aftermath. I told her that she would meet her loved ones and an archetype of her belief, which in her case would be Jesus. I explained to her that she would have a light review, an opportunity to see her entire life played back. I told her that she would see the same review again with the additional anguish of seeing how her choices and reactions affected the other people in her life. After this shocking and enlightening perspective, she would go to the Plane of Bliss. This is an environment that allows her to contemplate her light review, to see what she had learned, and to see what had not been learned. Armed with this knowledge, she would begin to educate herself in order to begin constructing the specifics of her next incarnation. If you have the time and the opportunity to read Ramtha's book, *The Plane of Bliss*, to the person you are with, the language and the certitude in which it is written will be of great comfort to those who are in transition.

"I think that having land and not ruining it
is the most beautiful art that anyone
could ever want to own."

Andy Warhol
American Artist

Chapter 25

CONTROLLING THE WEATHER

"Can you learn to control the weather?"

On my return home from the 2005 Belgium Retreat and Assay, I was on a flight from Amsterdam to Seattle when the captain came on the speaker system and told us that we were about twelve minutes from Edmonton, Canada, and about twenty-five minutes from flying over the Canadian Rockies where they were expecting a bumpy ride. He even used the word "jolts" in describing the turbulent air. He told us we would be flying at an altitude that would give us the smoothest ride. He said we had some very heavy headwinds and this might add to the unstable wind currents as they pushed up against the sides of the mountains. I had been watching the speed of the DC-10 and it was averaging about 460 miles per hour, which translated to about one-hundred-mile-an-hour headwinds.

I had a video monitor at my seat and I was able to go to channel 27 and watch an animated picture of our plane as it crossed the Canadian province of Alberta on its way to the Rocky Mountains. We were "holding to" an altitude of 32,000 feet.

I have learned that everything physical is programmed and held in place by the mind of its creator. In order to change that program, one must know how to reprogram the program with an intent to alter its physical characteristics. The wind, the mountains, a chair, a body, a chicken coop, and a river are examples of physical creations that are programmed and held in place by the last creator. I say last because if one knows how to change a physical object with a new intent, then it is held together by the new creator.

In World War II, it has been documented that those people and buildings that survived the atomic blasts in Japan were those who owned and lived in their homes. Those Japanese who were living in or renting someone else's homes did not survive. This is an example of being preserved within a home that has the intent of the owner who is living in it.

In Oklahoma City, a couple who had recently bought a house in a certain neighborhood renovated the bathroom as their first project in their newly purchased home. When a tornado swept through their neighborhood, the family jumped into the bathtub and pulled a piece of plywood over the top. When the storm was over, they opened the door of the bathroom and to their surprise the remainder of their house was gone and so was every other house on the block. The only surviving piece of housing was the newly renovated bathroom.

The captain had just told the flight attendants to stow the food and beverage carts and take a seat until we finished traversing the mountain range. I looked at my seat video monitor as the plane approached the mountain range. I have been taught how to reprogram or change physical matter. For the next ten minutes I focused on a symbol with this intent of changing the weather. I was able to place this symbol over the mountain terrain as it was depicted on my video monitor. The next twenty minutes, the projected time to get across the mountain range, was so unexpectedly smooth that it appeared as if we were in a vacuum. It was difficult to even hear the sound of the jet engines, so apparent when you are trying to listen to a movie or talk softly.

Ramtha taught some of his students how to tame the weather. I have learned how to reprogram an existing physical condition and to program my intent into the new object. It is now possible to understand the phrase, "Tell the mountain to move and it will move."

"Is it true that rain dances create rain?

I have known of many that did not work. In the seventies and eighties in Marin County, California, there were many attempts to create rain during a severe drought. These were dances on Mount Tamalpais that were performed by native elders.

Ramtha taught a small group of advanced students to become masters of the weather. I was in that group and our first test was to create rain for our area of Washington State in 2001, a particularly dry year for the Pacific Northwest.

It rained so hard for several months that my son and others asked if I could stop the rain. In this case it was a beautiful group effort. Knowledge is always the precursor to extraordinary manifestation.

If you are interested in knowing the knowledge and the disciplines necessary for doing the things you have read in this book, I encourage you to contact the school.

Ramtha's School of Enlightenment
P.O. Box 1210
Yelm, Washington 98597
www.ramtha.com

To order:
These Things You Shall Do...AND GREATER

Mulai de Guise Publishing
PMB 113 1310 NW State Avenue
Chehalis, WA 98532

Telephone: (360) 740-8278
Toll Free: (866) 922-8278
Fax: (360) 740-9182
Web Site: www.mulaideguisepublishing.com